VANDE VASUDHAIVAM

Abhijit Naskar is the 21st century Neuroscientist and Poet who has been serving at the forefront of humankind's struggle against hate, intolerance. bigotry and fanaticism.

Vande Vasudhaivam

100 Sonnets for
Our Planetary Pueblo

ABHIJIT
NASKAR

Also by Abhijit Naskar

The Art of Neuroscience in Everything
Your Own Neuron: A Tour of Your Psychic Brain
The God Parasite: Revelation of Neuroscience
The Spirituality Engine
Love Sutra: The Neuroscientific Manual of Love
Homo: A Brief History of Consciousness
Neurosutra: The Abhijit Naskar Collection
Autobiography of God: Biopsy of A Cognitive Reality
Biopsy of Religions: Neuroanalysis towards Universal
Tolerance
Prescription: Treating India's Soul
What is Mind?
In Search of Divinity: Journey to The Kingdom of Conscience
Love, God & Neurons: Memoir of a scientist who found
himself by getting lost
The Islamophobic Civilization: Voyage of Acceptance
Neurons of Jesus: Mind of A Teacher, Spouse & Thinker
Neurons, Oxygen & Nanak
The Education Decree
Principia Humanitas
The Krishna Cancer
Rowdy Buddha: The First Sapiens
We Are All Black: A Treatise on Racism
The Bengal Tigress: A Treatise on Gender Equality
Either Civilized or Phobic: A Treatise on Homosexuality
Wise Mating: A Treatise on Monogamy
Illusion of Religion: A Treatise on Religious
Fundamentalism
The Film Testament
Human Making is Our Mission: A Treatise on Parenting
I Am The Thread: My Mission
7 Billion Gods: Humans Above All
Lord is My Sheep: Gospel of Human
Morality Absolute
A Push in Perception
Let The Poor Be Your God
Conscience over Nonsense
Saint of The Sapiens
Time to Save Medicine

Fabric of Humanity
Build Bridges not Walls: In the name of Americana
The Constitution of The United Peoples of Earth
Lives to Serve Before I Sleep
When Humans Unite: Making A World Without Borders
All For Acceptance
Monk Meets World
Mission Reality
Citizens of Peace: Beyond The Savagery of Sovereignty
Operation Justice: To Make A Society That Needs No Law
See No Gender
The Gospel of Technology
Every Generation Needs Caretakers: The Gospel of
Patriotism
Aşkanjali: The Sufi Sermon
Mad About Humans: World Maker's Almanac
Revolution Indomable
When Call The People: My World My Responsibility
No Foreigner Only Family
Hurricane Humans: Give me accountability, I'll give you
peace
Ain't Enough to Look Human
Servitude is Sanctitude
Time To End Democracy: The Meritocratic Manifesto
I Vicdansaadet Speaking: No Rest Till The World is Lifted
Boldly Comes Justice: Sentient not Silent
Good Scientist: When Science and Service Combine
Sleepless for Society
Neden Türk: The Gospel of Secularism
Martyr Meets World: To Solve The Hard Problem of
Inhumanity
The Shape of A Human: Our America Their America
When Veins Ignite: Either Integration or Degradation
Heart Force One: Need No Gun to Defend Society
Solo Standing on Guard: Life Before Law
Generation Corazon: Nationalism is Terrorism
Mucize Insan: When The World is Family
Hometown Human: To Live For Soil and Society
Girl Over God: The Novel (Abi Naskar Adventures Book 1)
Gente Mente Adelante: Prejudice Conquered is World
Conquered
Earthquakin' Egalitarian: I Die Everyday So Your Children
Can Live
Giants in Jeans: 100 Sonnets of United Earth

Vatican Virus: The Forbidden Fiction (Abi Naskar
Adventures Book 2)
Karadeniz Chronicle: The Novel (Abi Naskar Adventures
Book 3)
Şehit Sevda Society: Even in Death I Shall Live
Handcrafted Humanity: 100 Sonnets For A Blunderful
World
Mücadele Muhabbet: Gospel of An Unarmed Soldier
Making Britain Civilized: How to Gain Readmission to The
Human Race
Dervish Advaitam: Gospel of Sacred Feminines and Holy
Fathers
Honor He Wrote: 100 Sonnets For Humans Not Vegetables
The Gentalist: There's No Social Work, Only Family Work
Either Reformist or Terrorist: If You Are Terror I Am Your
Grandfather
Woman Over World: The Novel (Abi Naskar Adventures
Book 4)
High Voltage Habib: Gospel of Undoctrination
Bulldozer on Duty
Find A Cause Outside Yourself: Sermon of Sustainability
Ingan Impossible: Handbook of Hatebusting
Amor Apocalypse: Canım Sana İhtiyacım
Amantes Assemble: 100 Sonnets of Servant Sultans
Mucize Misafir Merhaba: The Peace Testament
Divane Dynamite: Only truth in the cosmos is love
Sin Dios Sí Hay Divinidad: The Pastor Who Never Was
Corazon Calamidad: Obedient to None, Oppressive to None
Esperanza Impossible: 100 Sonnets of Ethics, Engineering &
Existence
Mukemmel Musalman: Kafir Biraz, Peygamber Biraz
Himalayan Sonneteer: 100 Sonnets of Unsubmission
Yarasistan: My Wounds, My Crown
The Centurion Sermon: Mental Por El Mundo
Her Insan Ailem: Everyone is Family, Everywhere is Home
Humankind, My Valentine: World's First Anthology of 1000
Sonnets
Aşk Mafia: Armor of The World

DEDICATION

*This work is not for the patriots of a nation,
it is for the patriots of a planet.*

Remember this:

*Heil Hitler, God save the king, Vande Mataram,
Patria o Muerte - it's all the same - a declaration
of tribal glory, with no concern for the rest of
humanity. Such archaic attitude suits a bronze-
age society, not a civilized one. It's time for
Vasudhaiva Kutumbakam (world is family), not
Vande Mataram (hail the motherland) - it's time
for Mundo y Vida (world and life), not Patria o
Muerte (homeland or death) - it's time for
Humans save Humanity, not God save the king.*

CONTENTS

1.   Preface:
World History 101 – The Actual History

ABHIJIT NASKAR

History is not a record of truth, history is a record of triumph. The triumphant writes history as it fits their narrative - or to be more accurate, history is written by the conquerors for maintaining the supremacy of the conquerors, while the conquered lose everything.

Let me give you an example. In a commendable endeavor of goodwill and reparations a descendant of the British conquerors, President Lyndon Johnson started Hispanic Heritage Week, which was later expanded into a month by another white descendant, President Ronald Reagan - fast forward to present time - during the Hispanic Heritage Month the entire North America tries to celebrate Native American history. But there is a glitch - Spanish is not even a Native American language.

Native Americans did not even speak Spanish, until the brutes of Spain overran Puerto Rico like pest bearing disease and destruction, after a pathetic criminal called Columbus stumbled upon "La Isabela" in the 1500s.

Many of the natives struggled till death to save their home - many were killed by the foreign diseases to which they had no immunity. Those who lived, every last trace of their identity was wiped out, by the all-powerful and glorious spanish colonizers - their language, their traditions, their heritage, everything - just like the Portuguese did in Brazil.

The Spaniards would've done the same to Philippines on the other side of the globe, had they had the convenience to stay longer. Heck, even the name Philippines is not the original name - the original name of the islands was (probably) Maniolas, as referred to by Ptolemy. But when the Spaniard retards of the time set foot there, they named it after, then crown prince, later Philip II of Spain.

Just reminiscing those abominable atrocities makes my blood boil, and yet somehow, the brutal "glory" of the conquerors lives on as such even in this day and age, as glory that is.

That's why José Martí is so important, that's why Kwanzaa is so important, that's why Darna is so important - in the making of a world that has a place for every culture, not just the culture of the conquerors.

No other "civilized" people have done more damage to the world than the Europeans, and yet, on the pages of history books their glory of conquest is still packaged as glory, not as atrocity. Why is that? I don't know the answer - do you?

Trillions of dollars, pounds and euros in aid won't suffice to undo the damage - but what just might heal those wounds from the past, is if the offspring of the oppressors and the offspring of the oppressed, both hand in hand and shoulder to shoulder, unravel the history as it happened, not as it was presented - what just might heal the scars of yesterday, is if together we come forward to learn about each other's past, so that for the first time in history, we can actually write "human history", not the "conquerors' history" - so that for the first time ever, we write history not as conquerors and conquered, not as oppressors and oppressed, but as one species - as one humankind.

2.   Humans Save Humanity
(Sonnet 1)

Sonnet 1

Heil Hitler, God save the king,
Vande Mataram, Patria o Muerte -
It's all a declaration of tribal glory,
That only makes our humanness fade away.

Such attitude suits a bronze-age society,
not a civilized one of reason and reform.
No more can we waste life on Vande Mataram,
Time has come for Vasudhaiva Kutumbakam.

Let us leave behind Patria o Muerte,
Civilization is founded on Mundo y Vida.
Instead of boasting moronities like monarchy,
Time has come for lucha por la igualdad.

God never saved none, for it's all imaginary.
That's why it's high time, Humans save Humanity.

3. The Great Engineer
(Sonnet 2 - 4)

Sonnet 2

Human welfare is human duty,
Intellectualize it not as politics -
Nor should you romanticize it as charity,
Why can't you be human without being elitist!

Why do you have to call it anything,
Why can't actions speak for themselves!
Place your attention on deeds not description,
Why do you gotta package it with a load of labels!

There is no politics, just our existential duty,
Organic life is predicated on certain responsibility.
While animal life demands shameless cruelty,
Human life demands fearless inclusivity.

Wake up o brave world engineer,
and reinvent the society!
Anybody can develop machines,
how 'bout developing humanity!

Sonnet 3

Not every engineer is humanitarian,
But a humanitarian makes the greatest engineer.

Be a living electronic circuit.
Practice resistance where needed, like a resistor.
Preserve energy where needed, like a capacitor.
Direct energy where needed, like a diode.
And above all, be driven by a purpose, like an IC.

Fanciest of life is existence wasted,
if purpose is unhoned.
Designing machine is easy,
using machine to design society
not so much, and there lies
the true glory of technology.
Spend enough time tinkering,
even you'll get the hang of it.

Bricks and brain can make a house,
but it ain't home without humanity.
Good engineer designs gadgets,
great engineer designs society.

Sonnet 4

4

Good engineer makes good innovator,
Great engineer makes social reformer.
Good teacher produces employees,
Great teacher produces employers.

Prepare for security so that
you never need to be insecure.
Place all attention on expansion,
and your light will never be obscured.

Pursue excellence, and you won't
have to worry about security.
Build your character and you won't
be incapacitated by insecurity.

Insecurity breeds fear, fear breeds fraudulence.
Pursuit of excellence is an act of truthfulness

4. Cheatcode of Life
(Sonnet 5 - 7)

Sonnet 5

ChatGPT Sonnet

ChatGPT is not a threat,
Any more than drugs are.
Ultimately it's just another test,
That helps strengthen character.
It is a helpful distraction that,
Reduces the competition exponentially.
As more boneheads use ChatGPT to cheat,
Worth of excellence will skyrocket globally.
Drugs used in moderation are medicine,
Drugs abused stifle health and sanity.
Likewise, algorithm used wisely is a boon,
Algorithm abused cripples life and society.
You can cheat in a few projects and exams using AI.
But there is no algorithm to help you cheat in life.

Sonnet 6

There is no handbook to life,
Only a fool thinks of fooling life.
That's why so few truly get to live,
Most pursue trivialities while alive.
Death is but an ancient myth -
Nobody who truly lives ever dies.
If you live today, you'll live tomorrow -
If you live, time lives, or else, time flies.
Life isn't about how many breaths you take,
Life is found in those you breathe life in.
Be kind and you'll live on in people's heart,
While cruelty makes you die every day as fiend.
Live now and you'll live tomorrow,
whether your body is alive or dead.
One who fears death is already dead.

Sonnet 7

I don't care for life,
I don't care for death,
I only care for immortality.
And immortality comes not through cheap thrills,
but by adding purpose to your mortality.

I don't care for booze,
drugs, God or government,
I only care for human upliftment.
I can accept anything and everything
that facilitates human welfare,
but I have zero tolerance for derangement.

My stimulation is music,
My courage comes from my backbone.
My religion comes from my heart,
In my brain my morality is honed.

You wanna get drunk? Get drunk
with an idea, not with alcohol.
Get drunk with alcohol, you ruin your life.
Get drunk with an idea, you enhance your life.

Nota: ¿Quieres emborracharte? Emborracharse con una idea, no con alcohol. Emborráchate con alcohol, la vida se arruinará. Emborráchate con una idea, la vida será mejorada.

Sí, estoy borracho, muy borracho! Estoy borracho con una idea - la idea de la unidad - la unidad de la humanidad.

5. Disillusioned
(Sonnet 8 - 10)

24

Sonnet 8

Drunkenness of alcohol ruins life,
Drunkenness of scripture ruins society.
Drunkenness of ideology ruins the world,
Drunkenness of nationality ruins humanity.

That is why, I avoid engaging with nationalists,
I avoid engaging with religious fundamentalists,
Not because I hate them, but because I don't
wanna hate them - not even my hatefullest critics.

Cut off all mindless ties to the past,
Live in the present for the present.
Shape your life in accordance with life,
Not by dead reckoning of habits and heritage.

Take life as your north star, not the dead.
Those who let the dead dictate life,
are digging their own grave.

Sonnet 9

Not all of history is primitive,
All time is a blend of terrible and terrific.
But you cannot tell what's good what's not,
Till you are disillusioned of all myth.

Disillusion yourself, my friend,
For the world has lost its way.
Stand your ground correcting yourself,
Watching you others will find the human way.

Embolden your senses to such an extent,
That you become a compass to the world.
It's okay if the world loses its way,
Never let their prejudice contaminate your heart.

Defy storms, defy disasters,
defy all torment of ignorance.
Whenever they peddle
superstitions as knowledge,
Break out as dinosaur,
and be the epitome of sentience.

Sonnet 10

When you accept all as equal,
you are not being broadminded,
you are just being human-minded.
When you do division as heritage,
you are not practicing tradition,
you are just behaving unsapient.

Sapiens life demands sapient behavior -
Life begins with equality, not breath.
Life moves forward with correction
of yesterday, not worship of yesterday.

They used to believe eclipse was an act of God,
Many still believe women are made to serve men.
If we still can't find flaw in these customs,
How dare we pathetic morons call ourselves human!

As I once said, it ain't enough to just look human.
An animal becomes human only by self-correction.

6. Westwashed
(Sonnet 11 - 13)

Sonnet 11

Women Run Better
(The Sonnet)

Men only inherit the world,
Women give birth to the world.
If women can birth the world,
women can run the world
(far better than men).

History reveals, war is a masculine merchandise,
Whereas preserving life is an act of the feminine.
Masculinity bears inclination for competitiveness,
Femininity is synonymous with synergy and cohesion.

That's why female leaders
can step down more gracefully,
making way for new minds at the helm,
Whereas their male counterparts would
rather take their position to the grave.

Femininity is not a reproductive quality,
Femininity is the source of all rejuvenation.
No matter what gender or orientation you are,
Nourish your femininity, and there'll be ascension.

Note: It's not enough to replace patriarchy with matriarchy, even though matriarchy is a far better alternative to patriarchy. We've got to build a society rooted in plain, ordinary, everyday goodness, beyond all caveman constructs of division. we've got to move beyond patriarchy and matriarchy - we've got to move beyond straight and queer - we've got to move beyond capitalism and socialism - we've got to move beyond east and west. In short, to build a world for the human beings, first we gotta behave like human beings - we've gotta behave not as western or eastern, but as human. Let's take the british empire for example.

Sonnet 12

Britain may have a few things to take pride in,
Conan Doyle and Doctor Who to name a few -
but colonialism is not one of them.
If you don't get this,
you are not a lousy brit,
you are just a lousy human.

Monarchy looks good only in one place,
on the pages of history books.
Dignity is earned, not inherited -
Any land that makes a mockery of dignity
declaring ruler by blood, is worse than crooks.

When your prosperity comes at the cost of others' ruin,
It is not prosperity, but proof of your primitivity.

Abundance rooted in exploitation is not abundance,
but evidence of your fraudulence and hypocrisy.

Better all head back to the jungle
than some fly in private jets
while others cry of hunger.
Better have no progress whatsoever,
than the rich get richer, and the poor poorer.

Sonnet 13

Autopsy of Western Advancement
(The Sonnet)

Poverty is a capitalist invention,
Third world obscurity is colonial construct.
History of the west is history of abuse,
World hunger is a western by-product.

How do you think the west made
so much advancement in so little time?
It's all by pillaging the innocent natives,
who welcomed them with nothing but smile.

Advancement can no longer be the prime objective,
We gotta advance without violating human welfare.
Unless we take off our shallow whitewashed glasses,
We can never prioritize life over almighty dollar.

The whole world is hypnotized by westwashed glory.

It's time for all humans to prioritize humanity.
Note: White supremacists boast about white americans being superior. Let's look at it reasonably, shall we - not that you can reason with fanatics!

Most of the third world speaks two or three languages, yet you say, white americans are superior!

Dreamers from the third world bear ten times more difficulty to achieve their dream, yet you say, white americans are superior!

Humankind's earliest scientific achievements came not from the West, but from the East and the Middle East, yet you say, America is superior - a juvenile

country whose very existence is rooted in humankind's worst of atrocities.

Well done! You really are superior - in cooking up fiction.

The fact of the matter is, excellence has no race. And the only inferior people on earth are the ones who think of others as such.

7. Masterclass
(Sonnet 14 - 16)

Sonnet 14

Masterclass for Humans
(The Sonnet)

Only the Native Americans are real Americans,
Everybody else is an immigrant.
Before you tell someone to go back to their country,
Start by heading back to Britain yourself.

Only Indigenous people are real Canadians, Kiwis,
and Aussies, everybody else is an immigrant.
Before you yell slurs at an immigrant of today,
Start by heading back to Europe yourself.

Turkey was transformed by one man,
Upon the foundation of thoughts most rational.
Before you bring back the days of fanaticism,
Start by taking down the statues of Mustafa Kemal.

India never had any organized religion,
Brahmin barbarians peddled a myth to have control.
Before you cremate a secular beacon into safron ashes,
Wipe out all memories of Kabir, Ambedkar and Tagore.

From discrimination to assimilation,
That's how we walk the course of progress.
Till every trace of intolerance is history,
Keep on struggling against mindlessness.

Sonnet 15

The Indian Sonnet

All through history India has provided sanctuary,
To the persecuted, shunned and alienated of the world.
Everyone from everywhere has toiled in India's making,
Many cultures beat together within the Indian heart.

Of course, there are peddlers of intolerance and hate,
Those who have been trying to build an extremist nation.
These primitive apes fail to think with their pea brain,
Of the word "hindu" the sanatana texts bear no mention.

The ancient citizens of India had no organized religion,
Life was just an expression of nonduality or undivision.
Indus valley is a rare land that assimilated all,
Without ever spreading the tentacles of invasion.

Many fervor, many faiths, thus India is made.
India without secularism is India of the dead.

Note: The best way to deal with a toxic relationship is to cut off that relationship. That's why I rarely write about the land I was born in. Better walk away from a toxic relationship than stay and turn bitter.

Sonnet 16

We Are Turkiye
(The Sonnet)

Earthquake may shatter our houses,
But it can never shatter our hearts.
We shall rise from the rubble once again,
We shall build back against nature's curse.

But this time let us build back better,
By putting our faith in science not politics.
We could've averted such cataclysmic terror,
Had we heeded the warnings of scientists.

A scientist works to preserve life,
Politician plays publicity with death.
Given the choice between the two,
Listen to the scientist without wait.

Why do people have to die
for us to open our eyes!
If we still fail to heed reason,
nothing will stop the funeral cries.

Note: Hanging pictures of a great leader on every wall doesn't make a nation great. Acting with warmth and reason against superstition and selfish interests, that's what makes a nation great. The problem with Turkiye is that, there are too pictures of Ataturk, and very few living Ataturks.

Biz Türkiye

(Bilim Adamının Şiiri)

Deprem binalarımızı yıkabilir,
Ama hiçbir deprem umudumuzu kıramaz.
Enkazdan biz yeniden yükseleceğiz,
Hiçbir felaket bizi köle yapamaz.

Gelin, milletimizi daha iyi inşa edelim,
Bu sefer siyasete değil bilime güvenelim.
Eğer bilimin uyarılarını dinleseydik,
Böyle bir felaketi önleyebilirdik.

Bilim insanı hayatı korumak için çalışır,
Politikacı ölümle politika oynar.
Herhangi bir karar vermen gerekiyorsa,
Bilim adamını dinleyerek karar ver.

Gözümüzü açabilmemiz için neden
insanların ölmesi gerekiyor?
Hala mantıklı davranmazsak,
cenazeler hiç durmuyor.

(Nerede niyet doğru,
Orada dünya doğru.
Hayvanların hükümeti yeter ya,
Bu sefer sadece Kılıçdaroğlu!)

8.   Earthwide
(Sonnet 17 - 19)

Sonnet 17

If I Were Head of State
(The Sonnet)

If I were the head of state,
my first act in government will be,
to dissolve the government,
and redistribute all powers of society,
to experts in their respective fields.

Civil servants and experts run a nation anyway,
While brainless politicians take all the credit.
Time to give credit and power where they're due,
Putting an end to the circus of representatives.

Instead of trading one incompetent fool for another,
We gotta rotate the civil servants office to office.
In a civilized democracy, civilians are the law,
Never you forget that, never let anyone forget it!

If I were the head of state, that is the end of state.
Dictatorships empower leaders, democracy empowers citizens.

Sonnet 18

Either Western or Human
(Undoing Westwash Sonnet)

When the Brits invade a country,
It's called the march of civilization.
When refugees arrive in search of life,
It's dehumanized as illegal immigration.

When America recruits talents from abroad,
It is proudly boasted as headhunting.
When another nation does exactly the same,
It is hailed as espionage and IP stealing.

When America spies on everybody else,
It is sugarcoated as national security.
If someone so much as loses a weather balloon,
It is used to gaslight a nation into a frenzy.

To see the world as it is, first
we gotta take off our western glasses.
Look at the human world with human eyes,
only then you'll fathom justice and progress.

Sonnet 19

The world doesn't have history,
what we have is whitewashed history.
The world doesn't have progress,
what we have is westwashed progress.

Better progress slowly and stay human,
than progress swiftly and become machine.
Time it is to humanize the spirit of progress,
out of the prison of cold western thinking.

We need neither western nor eastern,
but human thinking spreading earthwide.
We gotta measure humanity on human standards,
not on the whims of straight, catholic whites.

Spread your wings far and wide
beyond all hemispheric hogwash,
only then your heart will beat
without the stink of tribal trash.

9.   Inconvenient
(Sonnet 20 - 22)

Sonnet 20

When all life is rooted in duality,
It is not life, but a recipe for war.
When all thought is bound as binary,
Such thought raises nothing but wall.

When all politics is rooted in partisanism,
Political science is but animal science.
When all vision is bipolar, it's not vision,
But an absolute cockup of conscience.

Cockeyed sentience builds a cockeyed world,
To undo the cockup we gotta treat our duality.
We don't need to lean left or right,
We just need to lean loveside as one community.

To hell with how our ancestors lived or not.
If we must be tribal, let our tribe be love.

Sonnet 21

Political Wildlife
(The Sonnet)

Easiest way to study animal behavior
without going on safari, is to sit
in front of a political debate.
Political salesmen are ideal specimen
of wildlife in their natural habitat.

Listen to all the howling and screaming,
Listen to all the brainless twatter.
You shall learn a lot about the brutal wild,
By watching the cannibals devour each other.

In the world of political haftwits,
Politics is just "left and right" affair.
Where all left and right come to an end,
There begins actual human welfare.

Partisan world is a loveless world,
where popular truth is but a lie.
We don't need to lean left or right,
it is time, human heart spreads human-wide.

Sonnet 22

Ignorance is bliss,
Knowledge is pain.
To know is to grow,
To grow is inconvenient.

Lack of a natural explanation does not constitute
proof of a supernatural explanation.
When you don't know the answer
acknowledge your ignorance,
and start working at the question.

Lines of hands
don't make destiny,
labor of hands does.
Planets in heavens
don't define welfare,
planetary oneness does.

Those without brain and backbone seek comfort
in myths of chakras, lines and planetary movement.
Cavemen who still bear such prehistoric beliefs,
rightfully deserve falling prey to conmen/godmen.

10. Soulmine
(Sonnet 23 - 25)

54

Sonnet 23

All Roads Lead to Aum
(The Sonnet)

God needs no man,
Because (hu)man is God.
God is a mythical lie,
Godliness is not.

Oneness is Godliness,
Godliness is oneness.
World without oneness,
is a manifestation mindless.

Oneness is the Noor,
Oneness is Kabbalah.
Oneness is Aum,
Oneness is Nirvana.

All roads lead to Aum,
Whether you speak sanskrit, latin or klingon.
Light up the noor at the altar of heart,
Finally as true sapiens a common ape will dawn.

Sonnet 24

Give up your chase of goldmine,
Labor in the caverns of soulmine.
You shall be rich where it really counts,
Beyond the dreams of animalkind.

Soul by soul the world will glow,
Heart by heart society will walk.
Pay no heed to slime that mock,
You talk the walk and walk the talk.

If you wanna be a writer - write.
If you wanna be an immortal writer,
write till you drop dead.
If you wanna be a human - help.
If you wanna be an immortal human,
help till you drop dead.

One act of silent kindness is far greater
than reading all the books of Naskar.
One act of silent kindness is higher
than all the howling prayers.

Sonnet 25

Be ordinary people,
Live amongst ordinary people.
Be moved by ordinary people,
Thus we become extraordinary people.

No mortal ever becomes extraordinary,
by looking down on people as dirt.
Be moved by ordinary people,
and you'll move the world.

People are my path,
People are my purpose.
People are the heart of life,
People are the atlas.

People in my mind,
People as my map,
People are my freedom,
People are my trap.

11. Mean Well
(Sonnet 26 - 28)

Sonnet 26

People are the way,
people are the key.
Enemy of the people,
is enemy of humanity.

That enemy can come from anywhere,
Sometimes state, other times faith.
Inhumanity bears no allegiance to logic,
It often comes wearing an intellectual head.

Science is much more than intelligence,
Those who know not what science is,
boast about the supremacy of science,
While real scientists are ever consumed
in the humanitarian application of science.

Science is a great responsibility.
To use it recklessly like a highschool bully,
is a desecration of this sacred force of humanity.

Sonnet 27

Explanation comes from outside,
Revelation comes from inside.
No matter the data you dump inside,
Mind must digest them well
to develop some useful insight.

Coherence comes from realization,
Realization comes from contemplation.
Contemplation comes from curiosity,
Curiosity is rooted in expansion.

Yet most absolutely despise expansion,
Because expansion is extremely inconvenient.
So they mock the torchbearers of expansion,
Mockery is their way of disguising incompetence.

Funny thing is, in their heart
they actually believe they mean well.
It's a sad state of affairs when
hate is peddled as salvation from hell.

Sonnet 28

To Those Who Mean Well
(Sonnet From A God)

Dear vermin of the greedy gutters of earth,
I permit you to live as your whims may dawn.
I just wish, expired cigarette buts wouldn't
show the moronic audacity to advise the sun.

I don't hate you for your life of greed and filth,
But the most you are gonna get from me is pity.
Apes who are alien to the concept of accountability,
Are no more significant than a termite community.

With all your googling expertise, how about you
spend some data researching the term "ambition".
Know your place, my dear armchair intellectuals,
Chimps should speak only when spoken to by a human.

To you who mean well,
your death is the end of your story.
My death is the beginning of a legend.

Note: For every single dreamer of the world who keeps struggling for their dream, despite being ridiculed and patronized by inferior, bronzeage apes every step of the way.

12. Paranoia
(Sonnet 29 - 31)

Sonnet 29

When a genius is mistreated in his nation,
nobody utters a single f-ing word.
When the same genius is adored as a god
by another nation, he is branded traitor.

Enemy of a dreamer is the mediocre public
of their own damn nation.
Don't utter a bad word at them, sure but,
don't stand silent bearing abuse and exploitation.

You do you - and to hell with
the termites of yesterday!
Second-hand apes can't help but mock,
even at the sight of the civilized way.

Cuss for cuss makes more muck.
Bear no grudge against a single being,
Live not for revenge but for a purpose.

Sonnet 30

Ben seni rahat etmeye gelmedim,
Ben seni berbat etmeye geldim.
Ben seni uyutmaya gelmedim,
Senin uykunuzu bozmaya geldim.
I have come to destroy every
last trace of your pride,
prejudice, fear, and fanaticism.

I have come to destroy every
last trace of the prehistoric you,
so that a new human can usher
into a new world - a kind world,
a curious world, a human world.

I have come to ruin every
last trace of your sleep,
that keeps you oblivious
to the troubles of society.

Paranoia is the opium of over-informed primates.
Renounce paranoia, observe facts, act with kindness.

Sonnet 31

Sonnet of Self-Diagnosis

Superstition is the opium of the ill-informed public,
Conspiracy is the opium of the over-informed public.
With ten minutes of googling every flipping flat-earther
feels and behaves like a reputable rocket scientist.

Human mind has a prehistoric predisposition of paranoia,
To counteract ignorance mind cooks up brilliant fantasies.
Thus scientific expertise succumbs to facebook expertise,
Facebook groups become authority on medical diagnosis.

Self-diagnosis is a modern day healthcare crisis,
Where the patient desperately tries to redeem control.
In trying to oust the experts from science and medicine,
Google certified society only heralds its own funeral.

Take people out of healthcare, and healthcare is dead.
Take doctors out of healthcare, and healthcare is damage.

13. Fantasy
(Sonnet 32 - 34)

Sonnet 32

Soneto de La Medicina

MEDICINA significa Misericordia,
MEDICINA significa Ética,
MEDICINA significa Denuedo,
MEDICINA significa Integridad,
MEDICINA significa Cuidado,
MEDICINA significa Ingenio,
MEDICINA significa Nobleza,
MEDICINA significa Amabilidad.
La medicina no es una profesión,
La medicina es una vocación sagrada.
Un médico promedio salva un cuerpo,
Un buen médico salva una vida.
Una vida salvada es una familia salvada.
Una familia salvada es el mundo salvado.

Sonnet 33

What is Medicine without empathy,
What is Medicine without ethics,
What is Medicine without egalitarianism -
Ain't no practice by humans but by pricks.

Coldness has no place in medicine,
Either you are cold or you are a doctor.
Medical dictionary can lie on pedestal,
A distant doctor is a dead doctor.

If you can't feel the difference
between a scalpel and a cleaver,
there is no difference between
a doctor and a butcher.

In the absence of doctors who care,
People flock behind fraudsters who pretend.
Till we humanize all practice of science and medicine,
Reason cannot cure those "alternative" derangement.

Sonnet 34

People don't want clarity and answers,
People want comfort and security.
People don't want reality and rationality,
People want reassurance through fantasy.

Once the mind finds a reassuring fantasy,
It bends facts to maintain the bubble's integrity.
Life outside the bubble causes discomfort,
Mind avoids discomfort with make-believe reality.

It falls on us minds of science and medicine,
to treat the being, not just the body.
If half the scientists and doctors behaved human,
superstitions and conspiracies would drop
exponentially.

Till science and service become synonymous,
Superstition will fester one way or another.

Sonnet 35

Every thought of spirituality
brings up angels and spirits.
Every thought of enlightenment
bring a load of supernatural rubbish.

That's why I stopped using terms
like spirituality and enlightenment.
Because their baggage of superstition
outweighs their benefits to sapiens.

Focus on simple virtues instead,
Cut ties with irreparable concepts.
Speak of virtue, act on virtue,
You shall have all the enlightenment.

Do away with the supernatural,
learn to say "don't know"
when you lack understanding.
Chart your course with curiosity,
defying all convenient romanticizing.

Sonnet 36

Natural is supernatural we have understood,
Supernatural is natural we are yet to understand.
Order is chaos we have understood,
Chaos is order we are yet to understand.

Reality is nature, nature is reality -
Perception of nature is perception of reality.
Purpose of belief is self-preservation, not truth -
Sometimes you gotta put yourself in harm's way,
to act upon the light of understanding and sanity.

But under no circumstances you must let
rationality undermine your humanity,
Just like, you must never let belief and custom
taint your soul with the filth of animosity.

Cut off all ties with the tradition of heartlessness.
Human you are only when
the heart is alive with humanness.

Sonnet 37

Cut off all ties with archaic concepts, I say,
But I am not talkin' about everything illogical.
In trying to advocate for the voice of reason,
Don't end up yet another heartless atheist intolerable.

Militant atheists are no more humanist,
than religious fundamentalists are religious.
Humanism means to acknowledge human frailty,
and stand by them defying all logic and facts.

God is not a question of science,
God is a question of human rights.
God is an imagination that provides strength,
When real friends turn their backs downright.

God is nature's antidote to suffering,
How puny are you to cure it with reason!
If you don't get this simple fact,
you need lessons on humanizing
your logic delusion.

15. Imagination
(Sonnet 38 - 40)

Sonnet 38

Everybody has imaginary friends,
My imaginary friend is my late teacher,
And I find it therapeutic to talk to him,
Whenever I hit rock bottom during disaster.

Quite like air, water and food,
It's something we humans need to survive.
Last thing this world needs is more war
to prove whose imaginary friend
bears the greatest of might.

An imaginary friend that elevates life,
is indeed a rightful aid to existence.
We just need to be super cautious that,
reliance on imagination doesn't cause impotence.

Keep your reliance to bare minimum,
Don't delegate your life to imagination.
Focus on the idea, not the image,
Use the idea to aid your expansion.

Sonnet 39

Trance of Totem
(The Sonnet)

This is my decree to my soldiers of the future,
Refrain from raising my giant lifeless structures!
Use the funds to build schools and hospitals instead,
Providing free/affordable education and healthcare.

Keep me alive in your heart, not in dead statues,
each one taller and more extravagant than the other,
Just so self-absorbed snobs could take the perfect selfie,
to declare an empty alliance with humanitarian behavior.

If you must have symbollic momentos of me around,
Keep them personal, humble and utterly non-extravagant.
Always remember, I am honored with your acts of love,
not with your thousand feet statues and chants unsapient.

It's a sad state of affairs, when virtues
gather moss upon the monuments of hypocrisy.
Break your trance of totem poles,
be the freedom you are meant to be!

Sonnet 40

Hometown Human Sonnet

Everybody loves Rumi,
I learnt his tongue,
So I could pick up where he left off.
Better than basking in borrowed light,
Is to be an original light to the world.

Everybody yells, viva la libertad,
I learnt el idioma, so I could
humanize the paradigm of revolution.
Everybody loves Indus valley diversity,
Annitiki munde anni shaashtralu nerchkunnanu,
So I'm never out of spice for my humanitarianism.

Everybody loves boasting about their culture,
I spent years making all the cultures my own.
Thus my strength was amplified a thousand folds,
My sight expanded beyond all norms of vision known.

Polyglots have more fun - there is no question.
When science, poetry and polyglottery come together,
That's the beginning of a paradigm bending revolution.

16. Unstable
(Sonnet 41 - 43)

Sonnet 41

Language is the highway to culture,
To speak a tongue is to live a culture.
There is no such thing as native and foreigner,
Modern humans must rise above such petty divider.

Fancy exterior is no sign of modernity,
Modernity is predicated on expansion of mind.
Exterior is never a reflection of the interior,
Yet in our single-minded pursuit of applause,
we've placed all our attention on a fancy outside.

Substance of character is rarely a popular phenomenon,
Yet without character all popularity coaxes degradation.
Chase popularity, and you shall end up devastated inside.
Choose purpose instead, and you shall cause illumination.

Illumination begins when you acknowledge ignorance.
Ignorance driven assumptions are no sign of sapience.

Sonnet 42

You cannot believe in science
like you believe in the bible,
Bible is a constant,
science is a process.

To believe in bible is
to accept it as flawless,
needing no correction.
To believe in science is
to believe in the process
of eternal correction.

I am a mind of science, I recognize error, then
endeavor to correct them with all my brain-potential.
I am also aware of the good the bible bears,
that doesn't mean I am blind to its disastricles.

Point is, literature of any kind
can teach us a lot,
But any text refuting scrutiny
makes the skull a vacant lot.

Sonnet 43

Humanos Uranio
(El Soneto)

Para mí, no hay padre santo,
no hay prostituta impío,
solo hay gente.
Para mí, no hay familia real,
no hay familia conserje,
solo familia de gente.

Para mí, no hay científico,
no hay laico, solo gente.
Para mí, no hay espiritual,
no hay profano, solo gente.

Para algunos somos hijos de puta,
Para otros somos hijos de santa.
Yo digo, somos caballería del corazón,
Somos todos un reactor de fuerza.

Somos todos humanos uranio,
extremadamente inestables,
pero extremadamente potentes.

Uranium Humans
(The Sonnet)

In my eyes, there is no sex worker,
no faith worker, there's just people.
In my eyes, there's no royal blood,
no working class, there's just people.

In my eyes, there is no scientist,
no layperson, there's just people.
In my eyes, there is no spiritual,
no profane, there's just people.

To some, we cause envious heartburn -
To others, we are divine ointment.
Awake, Arise, O Corazon Cavalry -
We are all uranium humans,
extremely unstable, but extremely potent.

17. Validation
(Sonnet 44 - 46)

Sonnet 44

Potential is universal, action is not.
Capacity is universal, courage is not.
Individuality is universal, integrity is not.
Intuition is universal, initiative is not.

Human bodies are rampant in the world,
Human beings are rather scarce.
Human brains are rampant in the world,
Human minds are rather scarce.

Everybody has the potential for greatness,
Very few actually manifest that potential.
Because it's easier to follow a laid path,
Than be the pioneer of a path oneself.

Greatness requires originality,
and originality is inconvenient.
Be original bearing difficulty,
and greatness will come
chasing your luminescence.

Sonnet 45

Abhijit The Useless
(A Sonnet)

At school I didn't even know the term neuroscience,
Yet today I'm a symbol of neuroscience and psychology.
As a kid I never even dreamed of becoming a scientist,
I just wanted to observe the underpinnings of reality.

After high school I failed my medical entrance exam,
Yet to the world I am a vessel of ethics in medicine.
I chose CS Engineering instead but soon dropped out,
Yet today I am the epitome of responsible engineering.

Failure and success are eternally entangled,
Masses fear them while legends feast on failure.
I never felt the urge for academic validation,
Yet today I'm regularly cited in Springer.

I never studied science in the pursuit of grades,
I accidentally became a scientist by doing science.
Grades and degrees are shortcut to social validation,
But when you are a pioneer pushing the frontiers,
all mortal validation turns null and void.

Sonnet 46

Pursuit of validation is the ruin of originality,
Originality bears no care for social validation.
But don't confuse it to be an act of narcissism,
Pioneers are too busy building to heed admiration.

Let scrutiny and validation come as they may,
Beyond reward and punishment you keep working.
Pursue validation, they'll keep rejecting.
Pursue excellence, validation comes chasing.

Grow so big with your work that validators feel
out of breath at the sight of your vastness.
You know why I do not do promotion for my work!
It'd be like the Himalayas promoting the Everest.

Excellence is excellence because it heeds no nonsense.
Either you chase validation and end up a doormat,
or you pursue excellence and become a legend.

18. Rebellion
(Sonnet 47 - 49)

Sonnet 47

All the time I am teeming with ideas,
But alone I cannot bring them all to life.
I've got to choose the ones with greater impact,
And dump the rest to possibly never see light.

Like, I have a wish to see my sonnets become songs,
But my time is better spent writing, not composing.
So I leave it in the hands of my braveheart soldiers,
They may integrate new mediums as they find fitting.

Expand, expand, and expand again,
There is no end to expansion.
And never ever let your love for me
stifle your rightful progression.

Your life is your decision,
though you may learn from another.
Be a sponge to all the good around,
wielding them you shall rise a reformer.

Sonnet 48

What this world needs is benevolent narcissism,
But only a reformer can fathom what it means.
In a world that runs on materialism and greed,
You need a bit of narcissism to never give in.

In a world full of either yesmen or shallow rebels,
You gotta foster resolve tempered by a firm conscience.
When needed keep quiet, when needed explode,
but remember, obeying for no reason
and rebelling for no reason are equally mindless.

Sometimes quietude brings peace,
other times peace demands rebellion.
You gotta have conscience and character
to observe the requirement of the situation.

Patiently nourish your conscience
and embolden your character.
Otherwise, neither compliance
nor rebellion will avoid disaster.

Note: Learn from every custom, every culture, every
tradition. Don't reject them right away just because you
are hooked on the excitement that you get by rebelling
against everyone and everything.

Sonnet 49

Ramazan Söz (Şiir)

Ramazan yani sabır,
Ramazan yani sevmek.
Ramazan yani saadet,
Ramazan yani rahmet.

Ramazan bize umut verir,
Ramazan yapar cesur.
Hadi gelin, bayram edelim,
Affedelim her geçmiş kusur.

Ramazan yani bir ilahi söz,
Rahmetten vazgeçmem, söz verdim.
Bu ramazan ve her ramazan,
İnsanın evine insana hoş geldin.

Ramadan Promise
(The Sonnet)

Ramadan is an act of patience,
Ramadan is an act of care.
Ramadan bestows us with resilience,
Ramadan teaches us to share.

Ramadan is rejuvenation of hope,
Ramadan is resuscitation of courage.
Let us take a step beyond differences,
Come one, and come all, let us celebrate.

Ramadan is resurrection of a promise divine,
Festival of one people is festival of humankind.
Ramadan is the end of all feelings unkind,
Ramadan is a human being a human's lifeline.

Rahmat is an act of azan,
Rahmat is what makes us holy.
When Rahmat and Azan manifest as one,
That's the beginning of Ramazan,
Christmas and Deepavali.

19. Good from Everyone
(Sonnet 50 - 52)

Sonnet 50

Exceptions aside, there is no believer,
All I see is a sea of deceiver.
Who deceive themselves by believing,
Obedience to God is the same
as obedience to scripture.

There is no point to divine contemplation,
if it doesn't bring you closer to people.
If they really find God, whatever it is,
there won't be any place for hate in the world.

Where there is hate, there is no God,
Because God is but a manifestation of love.
Faith, facts, all are but meaningless choir,
If you look down on others from a pedestal above.

Religion is an act of unification -
If it causes divide,
you're studying religion wrong.
Religion organized is religion gone wrong.

Sonnet 51

Discipline of the Sikh,
Enthusiasm of the Christian,
Brotherhood of the Muslim,
Nonviolence of the Jain,
Clarity of the Buddhist,
Groundedness of the Hindu,
Rationality of the Atheist,
Resilience of the Jew -

Take the good from everyone,
Mind expands through assimilation.
Past errors mustn't continue as tradition,
Oneness is divinity, division is damnation.

Being kind costs us nothing -
not being kind will cost us everything.
Life united is life divine,
life divided is life unclean.

Oneness brings wholeness, wholeness brings sanity.
Without a unifying wholeness, all texts are insanity.

Sonnet 52

I have zero tolerance for intolerance -
If you want me to acknowledge you as a human being,
first learn to behave like a human being.
Mark you, opposite of intolerance is tolerance no more,
Across tolerance it's time to be loving and accepting.

Harmony is not a question of toleration,
Because harmony is not a question, but the answer.
But only those with harmony at heart can fathom this,
While the rest are busy intellectually devouring each other.

Intellect is not the answer,
Belief is not the answer.
These only amplify what we really are,
Good becomes great, jerk becomes jerker.

Heart is the key, world is the lock.
You run seeking here and there,
while you are the start, you are the stop.

20. Cripple
(Sonnet 53 - 55)

Sonnet 53

World doesn't change because you mean well,
World changes when you behave well.
You behave well when you behave with heart,
There ain't no heart when you reek of label.

Labels are like training wheels,
At some point you gotta let them go.
Or else those crutches will keep you a cripple
for the rest of your life as slave to woe.

Heart labeled is heart crippled,
Heart crippled is world crippled.
Denounce your crutches and walk on your feet,
And you shall rise rejuvenated self-enabled.

To name me is to maim me,
To inflame me is to inhale me.
In a world so native yet foreign,
I am just a Visvadesi (global native).

Sonnet 54

All forces of nature are Visvadesi,
Only insects of the gutter have nationality.
That's why I got no need for some grand promotion,
Elements of nature are intrinsic to all humanity.

The sun doesn't do promotion for its light,
Why should I!
The sun doesn't ask for recognition,
Why should I!

My light is infinite
because I care for no praise.
When you confuse acknowledgement
with achievement, and
applause with significance,
that's the end of your originality,
as well as your sweetness.

Focus on the work, not on
how it's accepted by the world.
Dream big and die big,
There's no honor in living as dirt.

Note: Everybody has a dream of how they wanna live, I have a dream of how I wanna die. I wanna die confronting bullets, not disease. Figure out how you wanna die, life will take care of itself.

Sonnet 55

Dreams come true not because
you are rich in money,
but because you are rich in persistence.
Circus animals are born
to spend their parents' wealth,
If you are human,
denounce all concept of inheritance.

Simplicity is my fashion,
Moderation is my trend.
There are creases on my shirt,
Because my heart is without bent.

Put an end to frivolities, and find yourself a purpose,
Legend becomes legend by burning the night oil.
You don't become great by chasing greatness,
Legend is born by toiling in the soulful soil.

When you choose struggle, you choose life,
Life of convenient complicity is mockery of life.
Comfort zone is coffin zone, wake up to life,
With a bold spine surf the time-bending tides.

21. Real Pro-Life
(Sonnet 56 - 58)

Sonnet 56

Coders awake,
Doctors awake,
Scientists awake,
Coppers awake.

Awake one, and Awake all,
The world needs your potential.
Take no worry, and shake all dread,
World of angst is world up the wall.

Break all walls of fear and divide,
Stand up firm with justice keen.
Others may stoop to all sorts of low,
You keep your backbone straight,
without any convenient lean.

Silence can bring peace,
Silence can breed war.
Choose your silence carefully,
Voice your mind to cause clarity
and end disaster.

Sonnet 57

Arise, O Atlas
(Sonnet 1100)

Vakna, Stå upp, o Modige Atlas!
Ta världen på din axel,
Förkasta allt som är ojust.

Awake, Arise, O Atlas Supreme,
Take the world on your shoulder.
Denounce all roots of hate and hurt,
Wielding your humanitarian viking thunder.

I don't write for creatures of gutter,
I write for those craving for open skies.
If you can give up your golden fancies,
I'll give you a world beyond the lies.

Despierta, levántate, oh loco amante!
El mundo entero está a tu cuidado.
Give up your aphrodisiac of wild ancestry,
Somos humanos cuando
nos descubrimos en cada humano.

Sonnet 58

When a species die more of disasters
of its own making, than natural disasters,
there is something fundamentally wrong
with that species despite the fancy exterior.

We gotta be pro-life in the real sense of the term,
Prioritizing life, not prejudice, dogma and decadence.
We cannot blindly draw measures of modern life
from a bunch of prehistoric documents.

For example, kids over cash, women over semen,
Of which only those with civil sentience can make sense.
Cavemen living in their biblical caves get but anxious,
Even at the thought of changing their prehistoric ways.

When norms are prioritized over life,
Such a paradigm is beyond repair.
Only way forward is to discard it altogether,
Even if it makes you a traitor to your ancestors.

22. Truth vs Facts
(Sonnet 59 - 61)

Sonnet 59

Intellectual ignorance and ignorant intellect,
Are both equally harmful to societal growth.
Problem is, we seem to fail at maintaining balance,
Either we are too logical or superstitious toad.

First and foremost you gotta be human,
Then be an intellectual all you want.
Unless you first humanize your priorities,
The intellectual is no better than the ignorant.

Human first, then all else,
That's the supreme civilized motto.
Mind not aware of this fact of life,
Is the root of all worldly woe.

Be love and be light -
watch the fall of worldly fright.
Be free and be responsible -
watch the society take its flight.

Sonnet 60

Sonnet 1103

Our ancestors are not the boss of us,
Life must be dictated by living conscience.
Dead people may have the right to make suggestions,
But they don't have the right to issue commandments.

Ancestors belong in history books,
Descendants belong in comic books.
Only we are alive to belong here and now,
Don't waste that life, submissive to books.

Too much involvement in the past cripples your present,
The same is true with too much involvement in the future.
If you are oblivious to the human condition now and here,
Ignorance and intellect will equally end up causing disaster.

Use past and future as markers of direction,
But never as authority on living tradition.

I don't make baseless claims like - I'll remove all your fears, I'll remove all your anxieties, I'll remove all your insecurities. I am a scientist, not an influencer - which means, I am dutybound to adhere to the truth, no matter how inconvenient they are, instead of peddling comforting lies for exposure. And the truth is, if bombarding people with some fancy facts about the mind removed their worries, every household with a DSM (Diagnostic and Statistical Manual of Mental Disorders) would be the happiest place on earth.

Sonnet 61

Only you can remove your anxiety,
Only you can bring you clarity.
What the hell are you doing
at the feet of fraudsters!
Go out and discover your own reality.

Your reality is at your own mercy,
But only if you are conscious enough.
Otherwise you'll spend life on autopilot,
Run solely on self-preserving instincts.

People run on instincts are easier to fool,
Hence the astounding boom in exploitation.

Feed people lies to comfort their insecurities,
And they'll shower you with admiration.
It's one thing to believe in someone,
and another to believe in what they stand for.
Believe if you must, not in me,
but in what I stand for.

Note: **I stand for truth, not facts.** Rationalists and empiricists may wonder, what's the difference? So, let's investigate further.

Truth and facts are not the same, because facts alone don't make the truth. Truth requires insight, truth requires wisdom. Facts can contribute to that insight and wisdom, but access to facts doesn't necessarily entail access to wisdom. The best example I can think of is that of love. Love is truth, whereas lust is fact. Lust may be a part of love, but it's not the whole of love. In fact, in many cases lust is not even part of the picture. The same goes for truth and facts. **Fact is a state of matter, truth is a state of mind.** Matter makes the mind - sure - but to fathom the matter behind mind in its fullest intricacies will take us millennia more.

23. Substance
(Sonnet 62 - 64)

Sonnet 62

Truth is a state of mind,
Fact is a state of matter.
Matter does indeed make the mind,
To fathom it will take us many more millennia.

Some facts have expiry date, some don't,
But truth is timeless, no matter what.
Pursuit of truth makes you humble,
If not, you are on the wrong track.

Truth makes you wise,
Wisdom brings you closer to truth.
It is an adventure eternal,
Facts are part, not the whole of truth.

Access to facts makes you an intellectual,
Access to wisdom makes you a sage.
While intellectuals peddle themselves as sage,
Sage remains an idiot unless otherwise requested.

Sonnet 63

When an expert doesn't know something,
They say, "I don't know", without tricks.
But an armchair intellectual knows it all,
Tiktok and Insta are their clinics.

An expert's worth remains the same,
with or without Tiktok and Insta.
Armchair intellectuals are here today gone tomorrow,
with the tiniest algorithm change of social media.

My work will continue,
with or without social media.
My work will continue,
with or without internet.
My work will continue,
with or without electricity even,
so will the work of every expert sapiens.

Instant popularity vanishes just as instantly,
Today you are relevant, tomorrow you are gone.
Make a real contribution that isn't overshadowed
by the next big tech revolution.

Sonnet 64

There'll always be a next big thing around the corner.
Question is, do you live your life biggest you can!
Again, I'm not talking about big in material abundance.
Are you using the fire in your veins fullest you can!

Make substance your aim, not exposure,
And you shall achieve great heights of excellence.
If you are constantly chasing exposure,
Today you are god, tomorrow you are garbage.

Be great or be dead, but the main point is,
Greatness comes when you are dead to popularity.
When you confuse greatness with fame and fortune,
You become stain upon your own sacred dignity.

Dignity is universal, yet very few use it.
When apathy becomes the norm,
backbone becomes an ancient relic.

24. AI - The Whole Picture
(Sonnet 65 - 67)

Sonnet 65

When backbone becomes a relic,
and sentiments inconvenient,
it's not progress but the
beginning of doom and derangement.

When over-mechanization cripples our growth,
When AI does all the thinking on our behalf,
You really think that's a sign of progress -
It's everything that sapiens is not.

In medicine, we have a condition
called oxygen toxicity,
which means, even oxygen can
do harm if inhaled excessively.

The same will happen in a AI run society.
Technology that started out to enhance capacity,
will end up ruining all the sweetness of humanity.

Imagine that - we usually associate oxygen with life, yet
that very oxygen can literally kill you if your lungs are
overexposed to it. The same is going to happen with our
brain from unrestrained use of AI. With the rise of AI,
machines may or may not become sentient, but one

thing is for certain - human mind will soon turn into vegetable.

We became an intelligent species by solving problems, and now that we are entering a technological era where we no longer need to solve problems on our own, leaving the key physiological functions of running the body, eventually the brain itself will become a vestigial organ, like the appendix. As we no longer need to think and act on our own, the cortex will begin to shrink, quite like unused muscle, and eventually, once again after millions of years, the primeval lizard brain, i.e. the limbic brain will gain full control of the new human animal. The rise of AI will be the end of "I".

But there is also another side to the picture. It's that, we cannot achieve much more, as a species, than what we already have, without the application of AI. So, the question is not whether AI is good for us - the real question is, are we mature enough to use AI for good.

And the straightforward answer is, no - we are not. Heck, we haven't yet got over our fetish for something so yesterday as nuclear weapons! That's why, the rise of AI will be the end of I - the rise of AI is the end of us. Please, I beg of you - let me be wrong.

Architecture is a reflection of the human spirit, poetry is a reflection of the human spirit, painting is a reflection of the human spirit. And difficult though it is to admit, modern generative AI can now do all of that on its own.

So the question is, do you want to live in a world where when you look around, the human spirit is nowhere to be found - not in poetry, not in paintings, not in buildings, nowhere! If not, then never trade in your originality for some two-bit convenience of AI.

Sonnet 66

Since there is no turning back,
So the real question is, how do we
use AI without destroying ourselves?

Here's how.

Use AI to enhance capacity,
not to avoid difficulty.
Use AI to accomplish tasks
that are otherwise impossible.
Prioritize AI to solve real-life problems,
not to make life more comfortable.

AI is ten times more dangerous than nuclear weapons,
Because repercussions of AI are way more far-reaching.
Unless we are careful with our exploits in AI,
Machine learning will end up a feat most dehumanizing.

All the tech in the world cannot make us better beings.
If we are better beings, can we use tech for humanizing.

Sonnet 67

AI can help us in harvesting data,
How we use that data is up to us.
All the data in the world means nothing,
If we don't use them to move together upwards.

Facts are easier to attain,
But truth not so much.
Yet most can't tell them apart,
Thus stupidity of superstition gets
replaced by stupidity of intelligence.

Facts are plenty,
but truth is one.
Messengers are plenty,
but the message is one.

Reason is plenty,
but the purpose is one.
Explanations are plenty,
but awareness is one.

Awareness is the cause,
Awareness is the effect.
Unawareness causes division,
Division causes descent.

25. Reflection
(Sonnet 68 - 70)

Sonnet 68

Don't be fooled by my attire,
You think of me a fool because
I want you to think of me a fool.
I am a behaviorist, and by behaving idiot
I study who's true, who's a tool.

I don't dress all ancient like a monk,
yet monks come to hear the words I utter.
I don't dress fancy like world leaders,
yet world leaders look to me for answer.

I don't wear the uniform of law,
yet coppers study me to be better cops.
I never got to put on a white coat,
yet white coats study me to be better docs.

I am the person beyond the paradigm,
I am but a reflection of the best of humankind.

Sonnet 69

You reflect my light,
I reflect your light.
When I am blue it darkens your mood,
When you're down I'm drowned in night.

Our mutual vulnerability is our greatest strength,
Across all insecurity let us be vulnerable together.
In hopelessness we are each other's compass,
In vulnerability we are each other's vigor.

That's why we gotta do away with ridicule,
We gotta do away with condescension.
Speak not foul, if you can't say something good
about someone who does no harm.

Progress is a series of reflections,
Each reflection is an effect as well as the cause.

Sonnet 70

I may share pictures, meeting people,
But I never share pictures, helping people.
Kindness is reward in itself to be savored,
Kindness with selfie is shallowness despicable.

The greatest humanitarians are silent humanitarians,
Who live their mission with zero claim to applause.
While populist charity is but a photo opportunity,
Real kindness needs neither approval nor applause.

When economic prosperity is rooted in disparity,
Prosperity of one leads to poverty of the rest.
When luxury is priority, disparity is imminent,
Charity becomes an act of guilt, not kindness.

Act kind or crave credit, you can't do both!
If you really care for economic justice,
start by taking the simplicity oath.

26. Rotten
(Sonnet 71 - 73)

Sonnet 71

80 percent of the things we buy,
are not because we need them,
but because our subconscious
mind is trying to fill an
unfillable hole in our life.

We live in a world that confuses material
abundance with economic prosperity,
But at the same time, material abundance
is actually a marker of mental deterioration.
So the question is, how do we maintain
economic as well as mental wellbeing,
without compromising either of them?

The answer is, through moderation.

Moderation is the key to sustainable health,
Moderation is the key to sustainable economy.
Yet moderation is frowned upon as alien and cheap,
Then they yell, why is there so much disparity!

Disparity and luxury go hand in hand,
Cut off luxury, you cut off disparity.
Until all have access to life essentials,
Nobody has the right to luxury.

Sonnet 72

Luxury is the enemy of growth,
Luxury is the enemy of ascension.
Excellence comes through moderation,
Abundance brings only degradation.

What's more concerning - mental health
deteriorates in direct proportion to materialism.
Abundance without accountability,
is recipe for extinction.

The reason is, we are an immature species,
Imagine an adult body with a child's mind.
We grew stronger on the outside,
without growing wiser on the inside.

Take control of your inside rottenness,
the outside will take care of itself.

Sonnet 73

Mind is a majestic blend
of rottenness and radiance,
Once you tame your rottenness,
lo, cracks your blinding radiance.

Eyes open or shut, doesn't matter,
Mind shut is the world shut.
Take your eyes past the eyes,
Mind will find its way to the heart.

Steal me from myself,
For I am now beyond help.
I want no peace, I want no lease,
Without purpose peace is hell.

Vessels are many, mission is just one.
When all burn with the habit of hateful divide,
Someone's gotta bring illumination.

27. Cement
(Sonnet 74 - 76)

Sonnet 74

To win the world, first you gotta
contain the world in your chest.
Compromise no dream to please the world,
Conquer your dream, the world will come to your aid.

Please the society, you ruin yourself,
as well as your society.
With middle finger to opinions,
keep at your ambition most ardently.

Time never remembers those who compromise,
Time only honors those with backbone of titanium.
Never you entertain shallow masses seeking
cheap justification for their impotence -
There is no advancement if there is no ambition.

Let them keep their opinions,
You keep your ambition.

Sonnet 75

World's salvation depends on your ambition,
Fate of the world depends on your fervor.
But if you wanna live like rest of the rats,
Be prepared for an existence most bitter.

Sweetness comes through freedom of fervor,
Fervor restrained by rigidity is most uncivilized.
Free fervor tempered by conscience alone,
Will pave the way for a world actually civilized.

Conscience is the cement
that settles character in place.
Character is the cement
that settles civilization in place.

Conscience, courage, compassion,
Behold the cornerstones of civilization.
All the sophistication counts for nothing,
If these three disappear from your vision.

Sonnet 76

Social norms apply to those without character,
Develop your character, and you become
the cornerstone of society,
As such you make the rules for society,
not the other way around.

For once in your life,
think for yourself,
How long will you live second-hand,
out of your ancestral basement?

Think, feel, live out of your own capacity -
If not, don't call yourself human.
The sun doesn't need permission to shine -
It just shines, and others rearrange
their lives to adjust to the sun.

Everybody likes to get a place of their own,
But very few foster a mind of their own.
They rebel for the wrong reasons at the wrong places,
Where it really counts they act the same old moron.

28. Excuse
(Sonnet 77 - 79)

Sonnet 77

To be original you gotta rebel,
But to rebel is not original.
When most rebel to seek attention,
It does nothing to reform the jungle.

Reform requires rebellion,
But rebellion is just a by-product.
Main thing is the act of uncompromise,
Which appears as rebellion to others.

In the mind of the reformer,
there is no rebellion, only reform.
It's an entirely different perspective,
vision is the line between rebellion and reform.

Rebel is a shallow word,
most times it's a sign of shallowness.
Find your mission, live your mission,
leave image analysis to the savages.

Sonnet 78

You won't find me nowhere,
not until you learn to look,
not with eyes of cults and caves,
but with the eyes of destiny's cook.

You are sanity, you are sentience,
You are the lifeforce of destiny.
You are conscience, you are concord,
You are the end of animosity.

There are three kinds of people in the world -
Those who make the world, those who mock the makers,
and those who sleep through all the making and mocking.
Or better yet, there are humans then there are animals -
Humans who make the world, humans who help the makers,
and animals are those who keep mocking and sleeping.

So the question is, are you a helper, maker or mocker?
Are you a spineless sleeper or a sleepless walker?

Sonnet 79

Sleep, sleep and sleep away,
One day you'll wake up in dismay.
You'll find, it is your last day,
And you spent your life in trivial play.

Entire life wasted in back-biting,
Entire existence gone down the drain!
With so much waste piling up,
It's hard to believe, we are human.

We are capable of so much,
We are capable of building worlds.
Yet we engage more in destruction than construction,
We use less power building bridges,
and more raising walls.

We just need an excuse
to commit mayhem and massacre.
Sometimes we credit it to god,
other times to law and order.

29. Breath
(Sonnet 80 - 82)

Sonnet 80

God is not an entity,
God is existence -
your existence, my existence.
But you cannot fathom this
with either faith or logic,
any more than you can fathom NYC
from Google maps.

Dear believer, I don't believe in an Almighty God.
Do you hate me for it? If yes,
you have learnt nothing from your faith.
Dear atheist, I don't believe in supremacy of facts.
Do you hate me for it? If yes,
you have no mind but machine, my friend.

Civilization is rooted in secularism,
Uncivilization is rooted in polar extremes,
like fundamentalism and militant atheism.

Many fervor, many faiths,
thus the world is made.
World without secularism
is world of the dead.

Sonnet 81

United we are alive,
Divided we are dead.
Integrated we're lovers,
Divided we are duffers.

It's okay to be daft in the head,
What's not okay is to be daft in heart.
The breath we share knows no divide,
Then why do we grind our sight in dirt!

Dirt is not a state of matter,
Dirt is a state of mind.
Mind with dirt is life of dirt,
Life of dirt leads to world unkind.

Together we care, together we dare -
Kindness turns air into breath,
Cruelty turns breath back into air.

Sonnet 82

Breath of the lungs is air,
Breath of the heart is care.
Defying all sneer and stare,
Living mind becomes life's stair.

It's okay if we move not fast,
It's okay if our mascara bleeds.
Head in hand, advance with heart,
Civil sentience ain't bound by creed.

Creed maps the ways of the past,
Conscience maps the way of the present.
Learn to walk free throwing maps in trash,
Mind is the only map you'll need for upliftment.

There is no map to the mind,
Mind is the map to time and space.
To draw a map you gotta be alive first,
Bury dead people's maps in dead people's graves.

30. Transcend
(Sonnet 83 - 85)

Sonnet 83

Worse than grave digging is grave dwelling,
Graves belong to the dead not the living.
Wake up to life with all your mind,
Be a whiff of fresh air amidst the dark tiding.

Humankind has made a habit of living out of graves.
All the isms, both old and new, are but gravism.
When claustrophobia is handed down as heritage,
Each generation sets off for degeneration.

But it doesn't have to be that way,
All that is needed is mind taking lead.
Honor the past, but honor more the present,
You are the charioteer, the present is your steed.

All our life we have lived in graves,
For once let us rise and taste the sun.
The sun holds the key to all that is dark,
Not the one in the sky, the one in our mann (mind).

Sonnet 84

Mind is the sun,
Life is the sky.
When clouds come to claim the sky,
Back you not so long as you're alive!

Be a crown to the future,
Not a doormat to the past.
You go make your own history,
Mould the present with mindful heart.

All reality is illusion -
Live in your own illusion,
don't live in another's.
Social reality gets humanized
by scrutiny generation after generation.

Forget about real unreal,
focus on human inhuman.
Forget about old and new,
focus on mental rejuvenation.

Sonnet 85

There is a difference between
transcending tradition and abandoning tradition.
There is a difference between
transcending religion and abandoning religion.

There is a difference between
transcending nation and abandoning nation.
There is a difference between
transcending culture and abandoning culture.

We transcend the sects by assimilating the sects,
This way we are empowered by all the good in them.
But if you abandon them blindly like a bonehead,
It is just a different kind of fundamentalism.

Intellectual boneheadedness is just as
primitive as fundamentalist boneheadedness.
If you can't tell the difference between
innocent fragility and harmful superstition,
all your intellect and logic ain't worth a cent.

31. Evernow
(Sonnet 86 - 88)

Sonnet 86

Cardiomyopathy Sonnet
(Medicine and Metaphor)

Person's worth comes from
their pulse, not from their purse.
It's okay if your purse is anemic,
so long as your veins got plenty pulse.

It's your pulse that brings the world to life,
Pulsating heart is radiator during this ice-age.
Ice-age never went away, it just got internalized,
As outwardly in appearance we became less savage.

Human heart is in dire need of a green house,
All the warmth is escaping rapidly.
Melting ice caps will drown us later,
We'll have kicked the bucket long before,
from frostbitten cardiomyopathy.

Brain's death is death of the body,
Heart's death is death of the being.
Kindness keeps the being alive
long after the heart stops beating.

Sonnet 87

There is no everafter,
There is only evernow.
There is no afterlife,
Just wake up to live now.

Now is timeless,
Now is eternal.
Now is existence,
Now is immortal.

Now has no birth,
Now has no death.
To live here and now,
Is a life sapient.

There is no everafter,
There is only evernow.
It's okay to spend some time in past and future,
But keep your feet rooted in here and now.

Sonnet 88

Roots are the seed of life,
Dead past cannot bear them.
Only the present is alive,
To bear roots and nourish them.

Life springs from here and now,
Past only adds some perspective.
If you live life on cavemen's thoughts,
Mind gets infected with horrible sepsis.

Keep the past in the past,
If you want to avoid infection.
Take the good, for sure,
But never ever without question.

It's not enough to put down roots,
We gotta put down roots where
life's welfare is the supreme tradition.
If you don't find such environment,
be the first to establish some ascension.

32. Honor
(Sonnet 89 - 91)

Sonnet 89

It's easy for an animal to be
yet another bigoted descendant.
It takes a human to defy descent,
becoming the hangman to decadence.

Amidst all the decadent descendants,
Be the ancestor to establish sanity.
Amidst all the dead meat of lethargy,
Be the first spark of life and liberty.

Life must first honor the living,
Then, if you want, honor the dead.
Welfare of the living must take preference
over welfare of the dead.

Live for life, live for the living -
Be blind, if you must, for those breathing.
Rejuvenate existence with a vision of life,
Hand-me-downs often contain
prejudice most crippling.

Sonnet 90

Exceptions aside, our ancestors were mental cripple,
They handed to us a world crippled by divisions.
We may accept their stupidity as part of evolution,
But we must never accept it as a sign of wisdom.

Love is wisdom, oneness is wisdom,
Impediments to these are sheer barbarism.
Foolishness of children is childish foolishness,
What it is not is mark of enlightened vision.

Our ancestors were children
on the evolutionary scale,
They might have had some good ideas,
but not all their ideas are acceptable.

Ancestry is expendable, acceptance is not.
If the dead teaches you exclusion,
Include the living, and leave the dead to rot.

Sonnet 91

Inclusion takes us forward,
Exclusion takes us backward.
Inclusion causes ascent,
Exclusion causes descent.

Yet descent has become heritage,
While ascent is deemed blasphemy.
Hence, you gotta stand your ground,
Otherwise no human will know humanity.

Descend you not to appease the dead,
Ascend you all for the sake of life.
Love, life and liberty, these are the mantra -
Liberty from rigidity, not from duties of light.

Light is accountability, light is responsibility.
My light is responsible for the light in you,
Your light is responsible for the light of humanity.

33. Coward
(Sonnet 92 - 94)

Sonnet 92

Yo canto en español,
Me encontré en español.
Español, el idioma de mi alma,
Fuente de mi fuerza, español.

Sana bir şarkı söyleyeyim,
Sana bir mektup yazayım.
Her şey seninle güzel,
İzin ver, seninle bir hayat kuralım.

I speak the tongues of earth,
I sing the songs of earth.
Forever I find myself,
In many fervors of earth.

Ain't got no single nation,
Ain't got no single culture.
Human am I, I belong to humans,
Come hell or come high water!

Sonnet 93

Mind inside and mind outside,
It's all one big conjuring trick.
Either step up as the mighty conjurer,
Or be enslaved by some primitive prick.

Harvest your mind well,
You'll reap the universe.
There's no triumph without torment,
Hurricanes are the harbinger of lovers.

We made so many excuses
to justify war and bloodshed.
Now let's foster the excuse for peace,
None may need more excuse to justify heartache.

There's a storm on the way,
Come all ye, who wanna join me!
Smiling let us castrate our doom,
Let us savor the catastrophe as candy!

Sonnet 94

Ain't No Coward
(Sonnet 1137)

Praying to be saved from danger,
Ain't no spineless coward I.
Let all the dangers hail my way,
Each crisis is like a trip to Hawaii.

Won't listen to no forbiddance,
Won't heed no foreboding.
None can sense the extent of my senses,
Night and day are my own making.

When all are eager for the sun to rise,
I grab the night and conjure up dawn.
Leave no corner of mindland unharvested,
Struggle isn't over till gloom turns to morn.

34. Unquenchable
(Sonnet 95 - 97)

Sonnet 95

So long we haven't hugged each other,
Aeon after aeon went without talking.
First strings of scripture
kept us apart, then g-strings.

All want body without strings,
Few foster mind without strings.
It means nothing to sleep without strings,
It's time we learn to think without strings.

Till your thirst of mind
outshines your thirst of body,
We shall remain slave to instincts,
Never to manifest our civil sanity.

Break the walls of mind,
just like you broke the walls of body.
Till you are free from all the strings,
Keep struggling against all deepseated ominosity.

Sonnet 96

There ain't nothing auspicious,
till we conquer our ominosity.
Till our dream of love overpowers
our excuses for hate,
fear is our deity.

The church is already within us,
Mosque, synagogue and temple as well.
All they lack is a rightful deity,
And what is higher than love unquenchable!

So I speak of love, I sing of love,
All my sonnets are but record of love.
My love isn't flattered by self-centricity,
For my love is too grand to rot in the tub.

Platonic, tectonic, animatronic, puritanic,
If you can't think of love without
thinking heavy machinery,
it's neither faith nor facts you lack,
what you lack is dignity and decency.

Sonnet 97

Vaishusmriti
(The Sonnet)

Those few afternoon trips back from uni,
With her head on my shoulder, were utopia.
My stomach was bursting with butterflies,
But my lips could barely utter a word.

My shirt got seeped with her intoxicating scent,
But her heart was posted to another man's mail.
Yet how can you begrudge someone you once loved!
It's okay to lose your heart to the wrong people.

Hadn't she rejected me, I'd have ended up
yet another nobody in the sea of engineers.
When life shatters you to a million pieces,
Get up and give back life some middle finger.

If you must love, love without any agenda,
If they love you back, your heart grows softer,
If they break you, your heart grows stronger,
Either way, in act of love there is no failure.

35. At The Helm
(Sonnet 98 – 100)

Sonnet 98

The only person who can defeat you is you,
Till you accept defeat there is no defeat.
Victory is not a matter of fate, but mindset,
Backbone primed tread danger under your feet.

Weakness in danger is insult on backbone,
Don't be weakened by imagination of danger.
Let the impulse of weakness come and go,
Don't be defeatist anticipating disaster.

There is no disaster mightier than you,
Be a disaster to all intolerant turmoil.
Even when your body is amidst concrete,
Keep your heart close to the soil.

To be an explorer of infinity,
First you gotta raise your anchor.
Unless you denounce the deadload of dogma,
You and the world are destined for disaster.

Sonnet 99

Naskar the scientist says,
Science that lifts no human condition,
is not science but superstition.
Naskar the monk says,
Inclusion is illumination,
discrimination is delusion.

Naskar the philosopher says,
Better lose truth, than lose humanity -
Better lose truth, than lose love.
Naskar the sufi says,
Sense yourself till
you sense nothing but love.

Naskar the humanist says,
I don't care about your belief or disbelief,
all I care about is your behavior with others.
Naskar the humanitarian says,
each human must earn their admission
into the human race with humane actions.

The spirit of love speaks of love,
no matter the faith and field.
Hate is but a mark of narrowness -
When you expand heart and soul,
whole world becomes kin and kith.

Sonnet 100

Sonnet 1143

Give me some sunshine,
Give me some rain!
Why the hell am I asking you,
When I'm the steward of my own reign!

Ship of society is sinking,
O Young and Bold, now hail the helm!
Come to the rescue of those lost at sea,
To hell with the nonsense of shame and fame!

My religion is to rescue the fallen,
My creed to care for the persecuted.
Faith, reason, nation, I heed none,
Obliterated in love heart is illuminated.

Shedding all fears both ragged and posh,
Let's go play in the courtyard of the cosmos!

BIBLIOGRAPHY

Archer M., (2000), Being Human: The Problem of Agency. Cambridge University Press.

Adolphs R (2003) Cognitive neuroscience of human social behaviour. Nature Rev Neurosci 4: 165–178.

Adolphs R, Tranel D, Damasio AR (2003) Dissociable neural systems for recognizing emotions. Brain Cogn 52: 61–69.

Andresen, Jensine, and Robert Forman, eds. Cognitive Models and Spiritual Maps. Bowling Green, Ohio: Imprint Academic, 2000.

Azari, Nina, Janpeter Nickel, Gilbert Wunderlich, Michael Niedeggen, Harald Hefter, Lutz Tellmann, Hans Herzog, Petra Stoerig, Dieter Birnbacher, and Rudiger Seitz. "Neural

Correlates of Religious Experience." European Journal of Neuroscience 13, no. 8 (2001)

Agar, N. (2004). Liberal eugenics: In defence of human enhancement. London: Blackwell Publishing.

Alteheld, N., Roessler, G., Vobig, M., & Walter, R. (2004). The retina implant new approach to a visual prosthesis. Biomedizinische Technik, 49(4), 99–103.

Bernstein R.J., (1971), Praxis and Action: Contemporary Philosophies of Human Activity. Philadelphia: University of Pennsylvania Press.

Bernstein R.J., (1976), The Restructuring Social and Political Thought.

Bernstein R.J., (1983), Beyond Relativism and Objectivism: Science, Hermeneutics, and Praxis. Philadelphia: University of Pennsylvania Press.

Bernstein R.J., (1986), Philosophical Profiles. Philadelphia: University of Pennsylvania Press.

Bernstein R.J., (1991), New Constellation. Cambridge: MIT Press.

Birkhead, T. R., Johnson, S. D. & Nettleship, D. N. (1985). Extra-pair matings and mate guarding in the common murre Uria aalge. - Anim. Behav. 33, p. 608-619.

Beauregard, Mario, and Vincent Paquette. "Neural Correlates of a Mystical Experience in Carmelite Nuns." Neuroscience Letters 405, no. 3 (2006)

Benson, Herbert. Timeless Healing: The Power and Biology of Belief. New York: Scribner, 1996

Bose, Subhas Chandra. An Indian Pilgrim: An Unfinished Autobiography, Oxford University Press, 1997

Bogen, J.E.(1995a), 'On the neurophysiology of consciousness: Part I. An overview', Consciousness and Cognition, 4.

Bogen, J.E. (1995b), 'On the neurophysiology of consciousness: Part II. Constraining the semantic problem', Consciousness and Cognition, 4.

Bremner, J. D., R. Soufer, et al. (2001). "Gender differences in cognitive and neural correlates of remembrance of emotional words." Psychopharmacol Bull 35 (3).

Brothers, L. (2002). The social brain: A project for integrating primate behavior and neurophysiology in a new domain. In J. T. Cacioppo et al. (Eds.), Foundations in neuroscience. Cambridge, MA: MIT Press.

Buss, D. D. (2003). Evolutionary Psychology: The New Science of Mind, 2nd ed. New York: Allyn & Bacon.

Buss, D. M. (1989). "Conflict between the sexes: Strategic interference and the evocation of anger and upset." J Pers Soc Psychol 56 (5).

Buss, D. M. (1995). "Psychological sex differences. Origins through sexual selection." Am Psychol 50 (3).

Buss, D. M., and D. P. Schmitt (1993). "Sexual strategies theory: An evolutionary perspective on human mating." Psychol Rev 100 (2).

Blakemore SJ, Decety J (2001) From the perception of action to the understanding of intention. Nature Rev Neurosci 2: 561.

Colapietro V., (1988), "Human Agency: The Habits of Our Being." Southern Journal of Philosophy, XXVI, 2, pp. 153-68.

Colapietro V., (1992), "Purpose, Power, and Agency." The Monist, 75, 4 (October) pp. 423-44.

Colapietro V., (2004a), "C. S. Peirce's Reclamation of Teleology." Nature in American Philosophy, ed. Jean De Groot (Washington, D.C.: Catholic University Press of America), pp. 88-108.

Carey DP, Perrett DI, Oram MW (1997) Recognizing, understanding and reproducing actions. In: Jeannerod M, Grafman J (eds) Handbook of neuropsychology. Vol. 11: Action and cognition. Elsevier, Amsterdam.

Carr L, Iacoboni M, Dubeau MC, Mazziotta JC, Lenzi GL (2003) Neural mechanisms of empathy in humans: a relay from neural systems for imitation to limbic areas. Proc Natl Acad Sci USA 100: 5497–5502.

Chomsky Noam, (2017) Requiem for the American Dream

Chomsky Noam, (2016) Who Rules the World?

Chomsky Noam, (2010) How the World Works

Churchland, P.S. (1986), Neurophilosophy (Cambridge, MA: The MIT Press).

Churchland, P.S. & Ramachandran, V.S. (1993), 'Filling in: Why Dennett is wrong', in Dennett and His Critics: Demystifying Mind, ed. B. Dahlbom (Oxford: Blackwell Scientific Press).

Churchland, P.S., Ramachandran, V.S. & Sejnowski, T.J. (1994), 'A critique of pure vision', in Large- scale Neuronal Theories of the Brain, ed. C. Koch & J.L. Davis (Cambridge, MA: The MIT Press).

Coyle EF. Integration of the physiological factors determining endurance performance ability. Exerc Sport Sci Rev. 1995;23:25–63.

Crick, F. (1994), The Astonishing Hypothesis: The Scientific Search for the Soul (New York: Simon and Schuster).

Crick, F. (1996), 'Visual perception: rivalry and consciousness', Nature, 379.

Crick, F. & Koch, C. (1992), 'The problem of consciousness', Scientific American, 267.

Damasio, A (2003a) Looking for Spinoza. Harcourt Inc. Damasio A (2003b) Feeling of emotion and the self. Ann NY Acad Sci 1001: 253–261.

d'Aquili, Eugene. "Senses of Reality in Science and Religion." Zygon 17, no 4 (1982)

d'Aquili, Eugene. "The Biopsychological Determinants of Religious Ritual Behavior." Zygon 10, no. 1 (1975)

d'Aquili, Eugene. "The Myth-Ritual Complex: A Biogenetic Structural Analysis." Zygon 18, no. 3 (1983)

d'Aquili, Eugene, and Andrew Newberg. The Mystical Mind: Probing the Biology of Religious Experience. Minneapolis: Fortress Press, 1999.

Daly DD. 1958. Ictal affect. Am J Psychiatry.

Damasio, A. (1994) Descartes' Error: Emotion, Reason and the Human Brain. New York, Putnams.

Damasio, A. (1999) The Feeling of What Happens: Body, Emotion and the Making of Consciousness. London, Heinemann.

Darwin, C. (1859) On the Origin of Species by Means of Natural Selection. London, Murray.

Darwin, C. (1871) The Descent of Man and Selection in Relation to Sex. London, John Murray.

Darwin, C. (1872) The Expression of the Emotions in Man and Animals. London, John Murray; also published

1965, Chicago, University of Chicago Press.

Dawkins, M.S. (1987) Minding and mattering. In C. Blakemore and S. Greenfield (eds) Mindwaves. Oxford, Blackwell, 151-60.

Dawkins, R. (1976) The Selfish Gene. Oxford, Oxford University Press; a new edition, with additional material, was published in 1989.

Di Pellegrino G, Fadiga L, Fogassi L, Gallese V, Rizzolatti G (1992) Understanding motor events: A neurophysiological study. Exp Brain Res 91: 176–80.

Deikman, A.J. (2000) A functional approach to mysticism. Journal of Consciousness Studies 7(11-12), 75-91.

Delmonte, M.M. (1987) Personality and meditation. In M. West (ed.) The Psychology of Meditation. Oxford, Clarendon Press, 118-32.

Dennett, D.C. (1988) Quining qualia. In A.J. Marcel and E. Bisiach (eds) Consciousness in Contemporary Science. Oxford, Oxford University Press, 42-77.

Dennett, D.C. (1991) Consciousness Explained. Boston, MA, and London, Little, Brown and Co.

Dennett, D.C. (1995a) Darwin's Dangerous Idea. London, Penguin.

Dennett, D.C. (1998b) Brainchildren: Essays on Designing Minds. Cambridge, MA, MIT Press.

Dewhurst, Kenneth, and A. W. Beard. "Sudden Religious Conversions in Temporal Lobe Epilepsy." British Journal of Psychiatry 117 (1970)

Dewhurst K, Beard AW. Sudden religious conversions in temporal lobe epilepsy. 1970 Epilepsy Behav 2003

Devinsky O, Lai G. Spirituality and religion in epilepsy. Epilepsy Behav 2008.

Devinsky, O., Morrell, MJ, Vogt, BA. (1995) 'Contribution of anterior cingulate cortex to behavior', Brain, 118.

E. Horvitz, "One Hundred Year Study on Artificial Intelligence: Reflections and Framing," ed: Stanford University, 2014.

Eckhart Meister, Selected Writings

Egidi R., ed. (1999), "Von Wright and 'Dante's Dream': Stages in a Philosophical Pilgrim's Progress", in In Search of a New Humanism: the Philosophy of G.H. von Wright, ed. by R. Egidi, Kluwer, Dordrecht.

Fadiga L, Fogassi L, Pavesi G, Rizzolatti G (1995) Motor facilitation during action observation: a magnetic stimulation study. J Neurophysiol 73: 2608–2611.

Fogassi L, Gallese V, Fadiga L, Rizzolatti G (1998) Neurons responding to the sight of goal directed hand/arm actions in the parietal area PF (7b) of the macaque monkey. Soc Neurosci Abs 24:257.5.

Frith U, Frith CD (2003) Development and neurophysiology of mentalizing. Philos Trans R Soc Lond B Biol Sci 358: 459.

Farah, M.J. (1989), 'The neural basis of mental imagery', Trends in Neurosciences, 10.

Freud, S. "The Interpretation of Dreams", 1900

Freud, S. "Selected papers on hysteria and other psychoneuroses" Journal of Nervous and Mental Disease 1909.

Freud, S. "The Origin and Development of Psychoanalysis", 1910

Freud, S. "Psychopathology of everyday life", 1914

Freud, S. "Beyond the Pleasure Principle", 1920

Frith, C.D. & Dolan, R.J. (1997), 'Abnormal beliefs: Delusions and memory', Paper presented at the May, 1997, Harvard Conference on Memory and Belief.

Gay, Volney, ed. Neuroscience and Religion. Plymouth, UK: Lexington Books, 2009.

Gazzaniga, M. S. (1985). The social brain. New York: Basic Books.

Gazzaniga, M.S. (1993), 'Brain mechanisms and conscious experience', Ciba Foundation Symposium, 174.

Geschwind N. "Behavioural changes in temporal lobe epilepsy". Psychol Med. 1979.

Gellhorn, E., Kiely, W.F. "Mystical states of consciousness: neurophysiological and clinical aspects." J Nerv Ment Dis. 1972;154:399-405.

Gray JA. The Psychology of Fear and Stress. 2nd ed. New York, NY: Cambridge University Press; 1988.

Gloor, P. (1992), 'Amygdala and temporal lobe epilepsy', in The Amygdala: Neurobiological Aspects of Emotion, Memory and Mental Dysfunction, ed J.P. Aggleton (New York: Wiley-Liss).

Greenspan, S. I. and S. G. Shanker (2004). The first idea: How symbols, language, and intelligence evolved from our early primate ancestors to modern humans. Cambridge, MA: Da Capo Press.

Grady, D. (1993), 'The vision thing: Mainly in the brain', Discover, June.

Gallese V, Keysers C, Rizzolatti G (2004) A unifying view of the basis of social cognition. Trends Cogn Sci 8: 396–403.

Guevara Che, The Motorcycle Diaries, 1992

Hari R, Forss N, Avikainen S, Kirveskari S, Salenius S, Rizzolatti G (1998) Activation of human primary motor cortex during action observation: a neuromagnetic study. Proc. Natl Acad Sci USA 95: 15061–15065.

Hardy, G. H. (1940). Ramanujan. Cambridge: Cambridge University Press.

Hall, Daniel, Keith Meador, and Harold Koenig. "Measuring Religiousness in Health Research: Review and Critique." Journal of Religion and Health 47, no. 2 (2008)

Harris, Sam, Jonas Kaplan, Ashley Curiel, Susan Bookheimer, Marco Iacoboni, and Mark Cohen. "The Neural Correlates of Religious and Nonreligious Belief." PLoS One 4, no. 10 (October 1, 2009)

Halgren, E. (1992), 'Emotional neurophysiology of the amygdala within the context of human cognition', in The Amygdala: Neurobiological Aspects of Emotion, Memory and Mental Dysfunction, ed J.P. Aggleton (New York: Wiley-Liss).

Halligan PW, Fink GR, Marshal JC, Vallar G. 2003. Spatial cognition: evidence from visual neglect. Trends Cogn Sci.

Handbook of Emotions, Edited by Michael Lewis, Jeannette M. Haviland-Jones, and Lisa Feldman Barrett, The Guilford Press; 3rd edition (2010).

Hameroff, S.R. and Penrose, R. (1996) Conscious events as orchestrated space-time selections. Journal of Consciousness Studies 3(1), 36-53; also reprinted in J. Shear (ed.) (1997) Explaining Consciousness-The Hard Problem. Cambridge, MA, MIT Press, 177-95.

Hardy, A. (1979) The Spiritual Nature of Man: A Study of Contemporary Religious Experience. Oxford, Clarendon Press.

Harre, R. and Gillett, G. (1994) The Discursive Mind. Thousand Oaks, CA, Sage.

Haugeland, J. (ed.) (1997) Mind Design II: Philosophy, Psychology, Artificial Intelligence. Cambridge, MA, MIT Press.

Hauser, M.D. (2000) Wild Minds: What Animals Really Think. New York, Henry Holt and Co.; London, Penguin.

Hebb, D.O. (1949) The Organization of Behavior. New York, Wiley.

Helmholtz, H.L.F. von (1856-67) Treatise on Physiological Optics.

Hess, EH (1975) "The role of pupil size in communication," Scientific American, 233(5), 110–12.

Heyes, C.M. (1998) Theory of mind in nonhuman primates. Behavioral and Brain Sciences 21, 101-48; with commentaries.

Heyes, C.M. and Galef, B.G. (eds) (1996) Social Learning in Animals: The Roots of Culture. San Diego, CA, Academic Press.

Hilgard, E.R. (1986) Divided Consciousness: Multiple Controls in Human Thought and Action. New York, Wiley.

Hilton, E.N., Lundberg, T.R. Transgender Women in the Female Category of Sport: Perspectives on Testosterone Suppression and Performance Advantage. Sports Med 51, 199–214 (2021).

Hitler, Adolf. Mein Kampf, 1925

Hodgson, R. (1891) A case of double consciousness. Proceedings of the Society for Psychical Research 7, 221-58.

Hofstadter, D.R. and Dennett, D.C. (eds) (1981) The Mind's I: Fantasies and Reflections on Self and Soul. London, Penguin.

Holland, J. (ed.) (2001) Ecstasy: The Complete Guide: A Comprehensive Look at the Risks and Benefits of MDMA. Rochester, VT, Park Street Press.

Holmes, D.S. (1987) The influence of meditation versus rest on physiological arousal. In M. West (ed.) The Psychology of Meditation. Oxford, Clarendon Press, 81-103.

Holt, J. (1999) Blindsight in debates about qualia. Journal of Consciousness Studies 6(5), 54-71.

Holloway RL (1996) Evolution of the human brain. In: Lock A, Peters CR (eds) Handbook of human symbolic evolution. Oxford University Press, Oxford

Jackson, F. (1982) Epiphenomenal qualia. Philosophical Quarterly 32, 127-36.

James, W. (1890) The Principles of Psychology (2 volumes). London, Macmillan.

James, W. (1902) The Varieties of Religious Experience: A Study in Human Nature. New York and London, Longmans, Green and Co.

Jay, M. (ed.) (1999) Artificial Paradises: A Drugs Reader. London, Penguin.

Jaynes, J. (1976) The Origin of Consciousness in the Breakdown of the Bicameral Mind. New York, Houghton Mifflin.

Johnson, M.K. and Raye, C.L. (1981) Reality monitoring. Psychological Review 88, 67-85.

Kadim I, Mahgoub O, Baqir S et al. (2015) Cultured meat from muscle stem cells: a review of challenges and prospects. J Integr Agr 14: 222–233

Kandel, E. R. In Search of Memory: The Emergence of a New Science of Mind, W. W. Norton & Company (2007).

Kandel E. R. Schwartz JH, Jessel TM. Principles of neural sciences. New York; McGraw Hill, 2000.

Kanwisher, N. (2001) Neural events and perceptual awareness. Cognition 79, 89-113; also reprinted inS. Dehaene (ed.) The Cognitive Neuroscience of Consciousness. Cambridge, MA, MIT Press, 89-113.

Kentridge, R.W. and Heywood, C.A. (1999) The status of blindsight. Journal of Consciousness Studies 6(5), 3-11.

Kihlstrom, J.F. (1996) Perception without awareness of what is perceived, learning without awareness of what is learned. In M. Velmans (ed.)

The Science of Consciousness. London, Routledge, 23-46.

Kosslyn, S.M. (1980) Image and Mind. Cambridge, MA, Harvard University Press.

Kosslyn, S.M. (1988) Aspects of a cognitive neuroscience of mental imagery. Science 240, 1621-6.

Kinsbourne, M. (1995), 'The intralaminar thalamic nucleii', Consciousness and Cognition, 4.

Kjaer, Troels, Camilla Bertelsen, Paola Piccini, David Brooks, Jorgen Alving, and Hans Lou. "Increased Dopamine Tone during Meditation- Induced Change of Consciousness." Cognitive Brain Research 13, no. 2 (April 2002)

Kölmel HW. 1985. Complex visual hallucinations in the hemianopic field. J Neurol Neurosurg Psychiatry.

Koenig, Harold. "Research on Religion, Spirituality, and Mental

Health: A Review." Canadian Journal of Psychiatry 54, no. 5 (May 2009)

Koenig, Harold, ed. Handbook of Religion and Mental Health. San Diego, CA: Academic Press, 1998

Kraepelin E. Psychiatry: A Textbook for Students and Physicians. New York, NY: Science History Publications; 1990.

Lauglin, Charles, John McManus, and Eugene d'Aquili. Brain, Symbol, and Experience. 2nd ed. New York: Columbia University Press, 1992

Lakoff, G. and M. Johnson (1999). Philosophy in the flesh. Basic Books: New York.

LeDoux, J. E. (1996). The emotional brain. New York: Simon & Schuster.

LeDoux, J.E. (1992), 'Emotion and the amygdala', in The Amygdala: Neurobiological Aspects of Emo- tion,

Memory and Mental Dysfunction, ed J.P. Aggleton (New York: Wiley-Liss).

Levin, D.T. and Simons, D.J. (1997) Failure to detect changes to attended objects in motion pictures. Psychonomic Bulletin and Review 4, 501-6.

Levine,J. (1983) Materialism and qualia: the explanatory gap. Pacific Philosophical Quarterly 64, 354-61.

Levine,J. (2001) Purple Haze: The Puzzle of Consciousness. New York, Oxford University Press. Levine, S. (1979) A Gradual Awakening. New York, Doubleday.

Lewicki, P., Czyzewska, M. and Hoffman, H. (1987) Unconscious acquisition of complex procedural knowledge. Journal of Experimental Psychology: Learning, Memory and Cognition 13, 523-30.

Lewicki, P., Hill, T. and Bizot, E. (1988) Acquisition of procedural knowledge about a pattern of stimuli that cannot be articulated. Cognitive Psychology 20, 24-37.

Lewicki, P., Hill, T. and Czyzewska, M. (1992) Nonconscious acquisition of information. American Psychologist 47, 796-801.

Mesulam MM, Mufson EJ (1982) Insula of the old world monkey. III: Efferent cortical output and comments on function. J Comp Neurol 212: 38–52.

Naskar, Abhijit. "Homo: A Brief History of Consciousness", 2015

Naskar, Abhijit. "What is Mind?", 2016

Naskar, Abhijit. "Love, God & Neurons: Memoir of A Scientist who found himself by getting lost", 2016

Naskar, Abhijit. "Principia Humanitas", 2017

Naskar, Abhijit. "We Are All Black: A Treatise on Racism", 2017

Naskar, Abhijit. "Either Civilized or Phobic: A Treatise on Homosexuality", 2017

Naskar, Abhijit. "The Bengal Tigress: A Treatise on Gender Equality", 2017

Naskar, Abhijit. "Morality Absolute", 2017

Naskar, Abhijit. "Build Bridges not Walls: In the name of Americana", 2018

Naskar, Abhijit. "Fabric of Humanity", 2018

Naskar, Abhijit. "Citizens of Peace: Beyond the Savagery of Sovereignty", 2019

Naskar, Abhijit. "The Constitution of The United Peoples of Earth", 2019

Naskar, Abhijit. "Neurons Giveth, Neurons Taketh Away | Abhijit Naskar | TEDxIIMRanchi", 2019 https://www.youtube.com/watch?v=BNX-Q0ySm80

Naskar, Abhijit. "Mission Reality", 2019

Naskar, Abhijit. "Operation Justice: To Make A Society That Needs No Law", 2019

Naskar, Abhijit. "Every Generation Needs Caretakers: The Gospel of Patriotism", 2020

Naskar, Abhijit. "Hurricane Humans: Give me accountability, I'll give you peace", 2020

Naskar, Abhijit. "Revolution Indomable", 2020

Naskar, Abhijit. "Servitude is Sanctitude", 2020

Naskar, Abhijit. "Good Scientist: When Science and Service Combine", 2020

Newberg, Andrew. "How God Changes Your Brain: An Introduction to Jewish Neurotheology", CCAR Journal: The Reform Jewish Quarterly, Winter 2016.

Newberg, Andrew, and Stephanie Newberg. "A Neuropsychological Perspective on Spiritual Development." In Handbook of Spiritual Development in Childhood and Adolescence, edited by Eugene Roehlkepartain, Pamela King, Linda Wagener, and Peter Benson. London: Sage Publications, Inc., 2005

Newberg, Andrew. "The Neurotheology Link An Intersection Between Spirituality and Health", Alternative and Complimentary Therapies, Vol 21 No 1, February 2015.

Newberg, Andrew, Nancy Wintering, Dharma Khalsa, Hannah Roggenkamp, and Mark Waldman. "Meditation Effects on Cognitive Function and Cerebral Blood Flow in Subjects with Memory Loss: A Preliminary Study." Journal of Alzheimer's Disease 20, no. 2 (2010)

Nash, M. (1995), 'Glimpses of the mind', Time.

Nesse RM. Proximate and evolutionary studies of anxiety, stress and depression: synergy at the interface. Neurosci Biobehav Rev. 1999;23:895-903.

Nicolelis, Miguel. (2011) "Beyond Boundaries: The New Neuroscience of Connecting Brains with Machines---and How It Will Change Our Lives", Times Books

O'Hara, K. and Scutt, T. (1996) There is no hard problem of consciousness. Journal of Consciousness Studies 3(4), 290-302, reprinted in J. Shear (ed.) (1997) Explaining Consciousness. Cambridge, MA, MIT Press, 69-82.

O'Regan, J.K. (1992) Solving the "real" mysteries of visual perception: the world as an outside memory. Canadian Journal of Psychology 46, 461-88.

O'Regan, J.K. and Noe, A. (2001) A sensorimotor account of vision and visual consciousness. Behavioral and Brain Sciences 24(5), 883-917.

O'Regan, J.K., Rensink, R.A. and Clark,].]. (1999) Change-blindness as a result of "mudsplashes." Nature 398, 34.

Ornstein, R.E. (1977) The Psychology of Consciousness (2nd edn). New York, Harcourt.

Ornstein, R.E. (1986) The Psychology of Consciousness (3rd edn). New York, Pehguin.

Ornstein, R.E. (1992) The Evolution of Consciousness. New York, Touchstone.

Penfield W, Faulk ME (1955) The insula: further observations on its function. Brain 78: 445– 470.

Penrose, R. (1994), Shadows of the Mind (Oxford: Oxford University Press).

Penrose, R. (1989), The Emperor's New Mind: Concerning Computers, Minds and The Laws of Physics (Oxford: Oxford University Press).

Persinger, "'I would kill in God's name' role of sex, weekly church attendance, report of a religious experience and limbic lability" Perceptual and Motor Skills 1997.

Persinger "Experimental simulation of the God experience" Neurotheology 2003.

Persinger, Corradini, Clement, Keaney, et al "Neurotheology and its convergence with neuroquantology" NeuroQuantology 2010.

Persinger, Koren and St-Pierre "The electromagnetic induction of mystical and altered states within the laboratory" Journal of Consciousness Exploration and Research 2010.

Persinger "Case report: A prototypical spontaneous 'sensed presence' of a sentient being and concomitant electroencephalographic activity in the clinical laboratory" Neurocase 2008.

Persinger and Saroka "Potential production of Hughlings Jackson's "parasitic consciousness" by physiologically-patterned weak transcerebral magnetic fields: QEEG and source localization" Epilepsy & Behavior 28 (2013).

Persinger. "The neuropsychiatry of paranormal experiences". J Neuropsychiatry Clin Neurosci 2001.

Persinger. "Neuropsychological bases of god beliefs", New York: Praeger, 1987

Persinger. "Temporal lobe epileptic signs and correlative behaviors displayed by normal populations", Journal of General Psychology, 1986

Perry BD, Pollard R. Homeostasis, stress, trauma, and adaptation. A neurodevelopmental view of childhood trauma. Child Adolesc Psychiatr Clin N Am. 1998;7:33.

Puce A, Perrett D (2003) Electrophysiological and brain imaging of biological motion. Philosoph Trans Royal Soc Lond, Series B, 358: 435–445.

Ramachandran VS. Behavioral and magnetoencephalographic correlates of plasticity in the adult human brain. Proc Natl Acad Sci USA 1993; 90: 10413–20.

Ramachandran VS. Phantom limbs, neglect syndromes, repressed memories, and Freudian psychology. Int Rev Neurobiol 1994; 37: 291–333.

Ramachandran VS. Plasticity and functional recovery in neurology. Clin Med 2005; 5: 368–73.

Ramachandran VS, Hirstein W. The perception of phantom limbs. The D. O. Hebb lecture. Brain 1998; 121: 1603–30.

Ramachandran VS, Rogers-Ramachandran D, Cobb S. Touching the phantom limb. Nature 1995; 377: 489–90.

Ramachandran VS, Rogers-Ramachandran D. Phantom limbs and neural plasticity. Arch Neurol 2000; 57: 317–20.

Ramachandran VS, Rogers-Ramachandran D. It's all done with mirrors. Sci Am Mind 2007; 18: 16–9.

Ramachandran VS, Rogers-Ramachandran D. Sensations referred to a patient's phantom arm from another subjects intact arm: perceptual correlates of mirror neurons. Med Hypotheses 2008; 70: 1233–4.

Ramachandran VS, Rogers-Ramachandran D, Stewart M. Perceptual correlates of massive cortical reorganization. Science 1992; 258: 1159–60.

Rizzolatti G, Craighero L (2004) The mirror-neuron system. Annu Rev Neurosci 27: 169–192.

Rizzolatti G, Fogassi L, Gallese V (2001) Neurophysiological mechanisms underlying the understanding and imitation of action. Nature Rev Neurosci 2:661–670.

Rock I, Victor J. Vision and touch: an experimentally created conflict between the two senses. Science 1964; 143: 594–6.

Rose´n B, Lundborg G. Training with a mirror in rehabilitation of the hand. Scand J Plast Reconstr Surg Hand Surg 2005; 39: 104–8.

Roberts, TA; Smalley, J; Ahrendt, D (December 2020). "Effect of gender affirming hormones on athletic performance in transwomen and transmen: implications for sporting organisations and legislators". British

Journal of Sports Medicine. 55 (11): 577–583

Royet JP, Plailly J, Delon-Martin C, Kareken DA, Segebarth C (2003) fMRI of emotional responses to odors: influence of hedonic valence and judgment, handedness, and gender. Neuroimage 20: 713–728.

Rozin R Haidt J and McCauley CR (2000) Disgust. In: Lewis M, Haviland-Jones JM (eds) Handbook of Emotion. 2nd Edition. Guilford Press, New York, pp 637–653.

Saxe R, Carey S, Kanwisher N (2004) Understanding other minds: linking developmental psychology and functional neuroimaging. Annu Rev Psychol 55: 87–124.

S. J. Russell and P. Norvig, Artificial intelligence: a modern approach (3rd edition): Prentice Hall, 2009.

Smith A (1759) The theory of moral sentiments (ed. 1976). Clarendon Press, Oxford.

Schilling, Vincent. 2017, indian country today

Stein, Stephen K. 2017, The Sea in World History: Exploration, Travel, and Trade

Simonsen R (2015) Eating for the future: veganism and the challenge of in vitro meat. In: Stapleton P, Byers A (Hg). Biopolitics and utopia. Palgrave Macmillan, New York (2015), S 167–190

Tesla N. "My Inventions", 1919

T. R. Society, "Machine learning: the power and promise of computers that learn by example," ed. The Royal Society, 2017.